THE LIMITS OF INDEPENDENCE

AMERICAN WOMEN
1760-1800

THE YOUNG OXFORD HISTORY OF WOMEN IN THE UNITED STATES

Nancy F. Cott, *General Editor*

THE LIMITS OF INDEPENDENCE

AMERICAN WOMEN 1760-1800

Marylynn Salmon

OXFORD UNIVERSITY PRESS

New York • Oxford

For Joe

Oxford University Press

Oxford   New York

Athens Auckland Bangkok Bogotá Bombay
Buenos Aires Calcutta Cape Town Dar es Salaam
Delhi Florence Hong Kong Istanbul Karachi
Kuala Lumpur Madras Madrid Melbourne
Mexico City Nairobi Paris Singapore
Taipei Tokyo Toronto Warsaw
and associated companies in
Berlin   Ibadan

Library of Congress Cataloging-in-Publication Data

Salmon, Marylynn
The Limits of Independence: American Women, 1760–1800 / Marylynn Salmon.
p. cm. — (The Young Oxford history of women in the United States ; v.3)
Includes bibliographical references and index.
ISBN 0-19-508125-0 (library edition); ISBN 0-19-508830-1 (series)
ISBN 0-19-512401-4 (paperback); ISBN 0-19-512398-0 (series, paperback)
1. Women—United States—History—18th century—Juvenile literature. 2. Women—United States—Social conditions—Juvenile literature.
[1. Women—History. 2. Women—Social conditions. 3. United States—Social conditions.]
I. Title. II. Series.
HQ1410.S25 1994

305.4'0973'09033—dc2O   93-30330
                                                                                          CIP
                                                                                          AC

3 5 7 9 8 6 4 2

Printed in the United States of America
on acid-free paper

Design: Leonard Levitsky
Picture Research: Pat Burns, Laura Kreiss

On the cover: Liberty and Washington, *circa 1800.*
Frontispiece: *A mid-18th-century wedding scene, embroidered in wool and silk on linen.*

CONTENTS

INTRODUCTION

I n the second half of the 18th century, a group of English colonies on the North American continent made themselves into a nation—a nation that was the first in history to establish the form of a republic among a numerous and diversified population. This process involved uniting and mobilizing inhabitants who came from Great Britain, Africa, and many European countries to carry on a war of independence from the British Empire, and it required implementing a form of government that had never before been tried in a large geographical area settled by people of more than one culture and religion. It also involved staking a grand territorial claim against the native peoples of eastern North America.

Women played important parts in the process of intercultural conflict and accommodation, in war, and in the invention of a new society that the establishment of the United States of America required. Their roles in the political realm were behind the scenes, for the political tradition that the founders of the American republic were establishing made the independent male citizen the most important actor. But women's creativity, adaptation, and cooperation were essential in households, in the community environment that supported the battlefield, and in the process of cultural change that enabled the forging of a new national identity out of disparate parts.

In an 1806 woodcut, a mother feeds her child. For most women of this period, caring for children was their primary activity.

The democratic promise of America at its founding encouraged the growth of some significant new opportunities for women, especially in education, as this book shows, even while the political role for women in the new republic was limited to their influence in the home.

This book is part of a series that covers the history of women in the United States from the 17th through the 20th century. Traditional historical writing has dealt almost entirely with men's lives because men have, until very recently, been the heads of state, the political officials, judges, ministers, and business leaders who have wielded the most visible and recorded power. But for several recent decades, new interest has arisen in social and cultural history, where common people are the actors who create trends and mark change as well as continuity. An outpouring of research and writing on women's history has been part of this trend to look at individuals and groups who have not held the reins of rule in their own hands but nonetheless participated in making history. The motive to address and correct sexual inequality in society has also vitally influenced women's history, on the thinking that knowledge of the past is essential to creating justice for the future.

The histories in this series look at many aspects of women's lives. The books ask new questions about the course of American history. How did the type and size of families change, and what difference did that make to people's lives? What expectations for women differed from those for men, and how did such expectations

Young women regularly produced samplers similar to this 1794 work to demonstrate their mastery of needlework skills.

change over the centuries? What roles did women play in the economy? What form did women's political participation take when they could not vote? And how did politics change when women did gain full citizenship? How did women work with other women who were like or unlike them, as well as with men, for social and political goals? What sex-specific constraints or opportunities did they face? The series aims to understand the diverse women who have peopled American history by investigating their work and leisure, family patterns, political activities, forms of organization, and outstanding accomplishments. Standard events of American history, from the settling of the continent to the American Revolution, the Civil War, industrialization, the U.S. entry onto the world stage, and world wars, are all here, too, but seen from the point of view of women's experiences. Together, the answers to new questions and the treatment of old ones from women's points of view make up a compelling narrative of four centuries of history in the United States.

—Nancy F. Cott

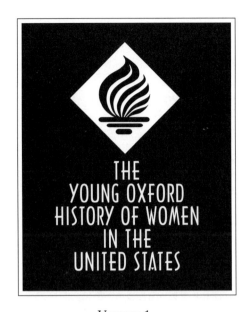

THE YOUNG OXFORD HISTORY OF WOMEN IN THE UNITED STATES

CHAPTER 1

TENSION ON THE FRONTIER: IROQUOIS WOMEN FACE A NEW WORLD ORDER

*T*he two women walked slowly through the cornfields, heading toward the forest that surrounded the village compound. Following Seneca custom, the younger woman had prepared a place in the woods to give birth. Now that her time had come, she was going there with her mother, a village healer and midwife.

The older woman followed the younger, who moved steadily ahead despite the pains that came every few minutes. She was well-prepared to give birth, for she was strong and healthy and, although this child would be her first, unafraid. Her mother had taught her the ways of women, and she knew that the pain of this birth, though strong, would last only a short while. She was confident she would bear her labor as a dignified Seneca woman should, without crying out. If she did give in to the pain, her people believed the child would suffer. Girls born of such mothers were known to be ill-natured, and boys proved cowardly in warfare. If her husband heard of her weakness, he would be ashamed.

They turned toward the sound of the brook that ran past their village on the eastern side and stopped a few hundred yards into the woods. The spot was close to their fields yet private, shielded on two sides by young hemlocks and bounded on a third by the brook,

A Dutch engraving gives a European view of an American Indian family.

where the child would be dipped soon after birth. The washing was meant not only to clean and stimulate the child, but also to harden it against the coming rigors of Indian life. The mother approved of her daughter's choice and the way she had swept the earth and covered the ground with pine needles and hemlock boughs. On the ground, they laid the blankets they had brought. As night was approaching and the season was cold, the mother built a fire to warm them.

The midwife admired the endurance of her daughter, who laid down only between her pains, gathering herself for the effort to kneel through each contraction. The labor was long because it was her first. Despite the fact that she had remained in the village throughout the entire first day of her birth pains, working on her pelts, preparing food for her husband, and helping care for her sister's children, the wait in the woods seemed long, too long to the mother. Toward morning, the mother decided to intervene and prepared a medicine to speed her daughter's contractions. She danced around the young woman, singing a special song to plead for help in bringing forth the baby. Soon her efforts were rewarded. With great determination the daughter rose to grasp the leather thong tied to the tree above her, trembling as she pushed her legs against the earth,

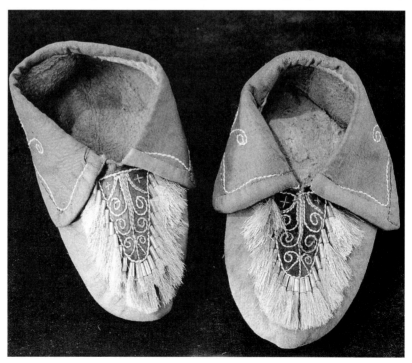

These deerskin moccasins are embroidered with porcupine quills and tufts of dyed deer hair in a characteristic Iroquois tree design. They were worn by an Iroquois child in the mid-18th century.

groaning as the infant's head broke through. After one final push, the midwife held the newborn in her hands. Her daughter lay back on the blankets, exhausted, while she cut the umbilical cord and wiped the baby's face clean. "It is a girl," she announced. "You have done well." The new mother held her baby and an overwhelming sense of joy and relief passed through her. The baby was whole and unharmed. She would grow up to be a great help and comfort, and the line of women in their family would continue, strong and uninterrupted.

Only a few hours after her delivery, the Seneca woman returned to her log house in the village. She held her baby wrapped in the beautifully decorated blanket she had made for it and displayed the girl proudly to the other women, children, and her husband. Her thoughts were on the family's happy future signified by the successful birth, but her mother's thoughts were much less joyful. She knew more than her daughter about the problems of their people, and to her the new generation seemed faced with more difficulties than they could overcome. Her pleasure at the birth of a granddaughter was tinged with sadness.

The Seneca nation of Indians, which controlled the region of western New York State between Seneca Lake and Lake Erie, would have included women such as those in this story. The Seneca was the largest and the most powerful of the six tribes that made up the Iroquois Confederacy. Seneca men ranged over a territory that extended from the Mississippi River east to the Atlantic Ocean and from Hudson Bay south to the Carolinas. They traveled to hunt and to conduct warfare and diplomacy, and often were gone from their villages for weeks or months at a time. In fact, Iroquois men were away from home for such extended periods that women came to control much of the day-to-day affairs of village life.

Among the Iroquois, women were the farmers. They produced the corn that was the mainstay of their people's diet and supplemental crops of squash and beans. Women also raised tobacco to smoke and herbs for teas and medicines. To add variety to their diet, they gathered fresh fruits, nuts, and insects such as grasshoppers.

Women usually farmed communally, although individuals could work their own plots of land if they preferred. They had little incentive to farm alone, however. Even if a farmer could produce extra food for later use, such hoarding would be frowned upon if other families in the village were in need.

The Iroquois had no concept of private land ownership. A woman might work a particular piece of land, and as long as she used the plot, it was considered hers. But when the village moved to another location, as it did from time to time, she no longer held a claim to her old fields. Near the new village she simply etched out another plot for her family. Economic security came primarily from contributing to the good of the village as a whole, rather than from individually owning and working a farm plot.

In addition to being the primary food producers for their villages, Iroquois women also maintained social stability through tightly knit female relationships. The mother-daughter bond was particularly strong. The Iroquois considered it more important than any other relationship, including that between a wife and husband. In times of trouble, women turned to each other for food, medical care, and advice on love and childrearing. The reason was simple: women were always there, whereas husbands, fathers, brothers, and sons were often away.

The close mother-daughter bond helped dictate where family

Native American women pound corn (left) and carry firewood near their longhouse. This sketch comes from a map drawn by F. G. Bressani in 1657, one of the earliest European depictions of Northeastern Indian daily life.

members lived. Traditionally, large Iroquois dwellings, known as longhouses, sheltered as many as 50 or 60 people, all descendants of one elderly woman. By the mid-18th century, however, smaller houses had become common. They often lodged only a single family or a mother and one daughter with her family. Unmarried sons as well as daughters lived with their mothers. The houses, then, and the fields that surrounded them, were controlled by the women of Iroquois villages.

Children also came under the control of women more than men. Infants and toddlers spent all of their time with their mothers because weaning did not occur until children were three or four years old. During later childhood, Iroquois boys and girls stayed in or around their villages, where they played and performed easy chores. Fathers came and went, providing essentials such as meat and trade goods for their families and offering instruction or advice as necessary. Although their contributions were important, they represented only distant figures compared to mothers.

After reaching eight or nine, boys came less directly under female control. At this time they began to imitate adult male behavior by forming hunting gangs that roamed the woods in search of small game. Until they reached manhood, these gangs maintained independence from both parents to a great extent. Older girls, meanwhile, remained with their mothers in the village compound, where they performed traditional women's work: farming, preparing animal pelts, caring for younger children, making baskets and pottery, and gathering, preserving, and cooking food.

Iroquois children of both sexes were reared indulgently. Mothers sought to harden their children by bathing them in cold water, but they rarely punished them for misbehavior. Parents assumed that by observing and imitating adult standards of conduct their children would outgrow unpleasant habits without much interference. White observers commented on the passionate love Iroquois women felt for their children and noted the mothers' refusal to strike or restrain them. Scholars believe the Iroquois avoided physical restraint and blows out of respect for their children. The Iroquois believed that children could be insulted as easily as adults, and parents wanted their offspring to remember them with love and respect, not fear and resentment. Perhaps as a result of the respect they were given as children, Iroquois adults often displayed a fierce desire to remain free and independent of all restraints.

The close and enduring ties of women complemented the loose and often short-term relationships between women and men. Men's frequent and lengthy absences placed a great strain on some marriages, and divorces and subsequent remarriages were common. A divorce could be initiated by either spouse, but often women entered into new marriages while their husbands were away from home. Because women were primarily responsible for the day-to-day care and feeding of young children and because land was held in common, questions of paternity and inheritance did not disrupt this system of remarriage.

Love, sexual attraction, and rejection were of great importance to the Iroquois. They readily consulted medicine women and men or even witches about problems in their relationships. Rejected spouses were usually encouraged to find new mates and accept the new unions of their former wives or husbands. Retaliation against a former spouse was discouraged largely because men's absences made easy divorce and remarriage a social necessity.

The clearly defined social roles of Iroquois women and men helped them deal with the tension of continual warfare between European powers in America. During the first half of the 18th century, France and England fought three separate wars for control of the northeastern interior and the vast wealth of the Indian fur trade. Throughout the conflict Iroquois warriors and diplomats never established a permanent allegiance to one side or the other. This allowed them to negotiate gifts from both nations in exchange for military favors. They also wanted to keep their people's freedom to trade wherever it was most profitable. As a result of careful negotiating, only the native inhabitants had maintained complete freedom to travel and trade at will. This delicate balance, in which the Iroquois kept two great European powers dependent on them for decades, finally was destroyed by Great Britain's increasing strength in the region. The English became determined to dominate the continent. In the French and Indian War (1754–63), England finally destroyed the French threat. After the war, France could no longer hinder the construction of English forts along the frontier or interfere with England's dominance of the fur trade.

This English diagram demonstrates how Indians killed beavers for the fur trade. Although they labeled the native people "savage," Europeans recognized their superior hunting and trapping skills and let them control that aspect of the fur trade.

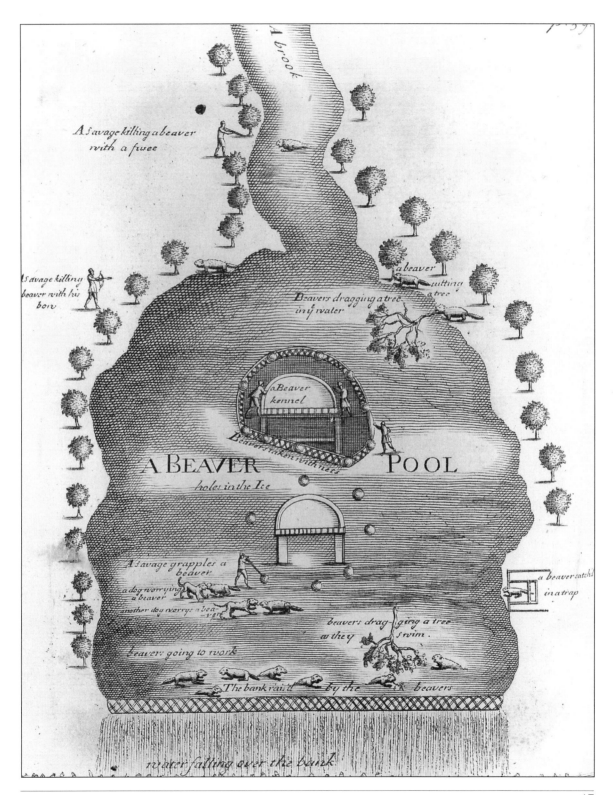

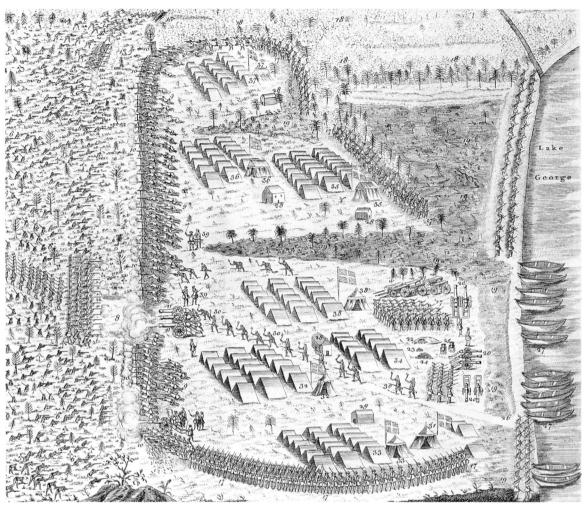

In the Battle of Lake George in September 1755, 2,000 English troops and 250 Mohawks defeated a combined force of 2,500 French and their Indian allies.

As a result of their victory, the English changed the way in which they negotiated with the Native American inhabitants of frontier areas. Because the whites no longer needed the help of tribes such as the Seneca, they refused to pay them rent for the forts they constructed in Indian territory. They also raised the prices of trade goods and refused to give their former Indian allies traditional presents of hardware, dry goods, powder, lead, and rum. The Iroquois had become dependent on these goods. Without ready access to them, the Iroquois way of life was threatened. Even more disturbing was England's decision to allow white settlers to move onto Iroquois and Delaware lands in the Monongahela and Susquehanna valleys. (The Delaware controlled western Pennsylvania.) The Indians could not tolerate such disrespect for their ancient rights to this land.

Traditional Iroquois ways gave both women and men the right to decide when to go to war. In Iroquois politics men did the public speaking and announced the decisions of the tribes in great meetings, but women freely exhorted the men to action or delay. The influence of individual women varied according to the persuasiveness of their arguments and their personal status within the tribe. English behavior after the war with France had so angered the Iroquois that both women and men demanded action.

An Indian uprising—named Pontiac's Rebellion after the Ottawa leader who instigated it—began in the spring of 1763. In addition to the six nations of the Iroquois Confederacy, it involved the Huron, Chippewa, Potawatomi, Delaware, and Shawnee nations and some Mingo (Pennsylvania Iroquois exiled to the Ohio Valley). The Seneca played a particularly important role in igniting the war, which they planned over a period of two years and to which they contributed many warriors. Initially, the Native American fighters had a series of striking successes. They destroyed all the British outposts in the Great Lakes region west of Fort Niagara and north of Fort Pitt (at Pittsburgh) and killed at least 2,000 white settlers along the Virginia and Pennsylvania frontiers.

The English never were in serious danger of losing control of the region, however. Forts Detroit, Pitt, and Niagara withstood attack, and eventually Indian supplies ran low. When English reinforcements arrived at the forts in the fall, the Indians gave up the fight. Pontiac was the last chief to lay down arms. His siege of the English fort at Detroit ended in late October, after most of the other Indian warriors already had given up and returned to their villages.

At about the same time that Pontiac was abandoning his efforts, the English government issued the Proclamation of 1763. This order recognized the exclusive right of the indigenous peoples to inhabit frontier lands previously controlled by the French. The English government recognized that without great effort it could not control the vast new territories it had acquired from France. Rather than risk continual warfare with the native inhabitants, it forbade English settlement in these areas. In theory the English proclamation line was an effort to prevent conflict until better arrangements could be made for the native inhabitants. In practice the idea was unworkable from the beginning, as many whites had already moved

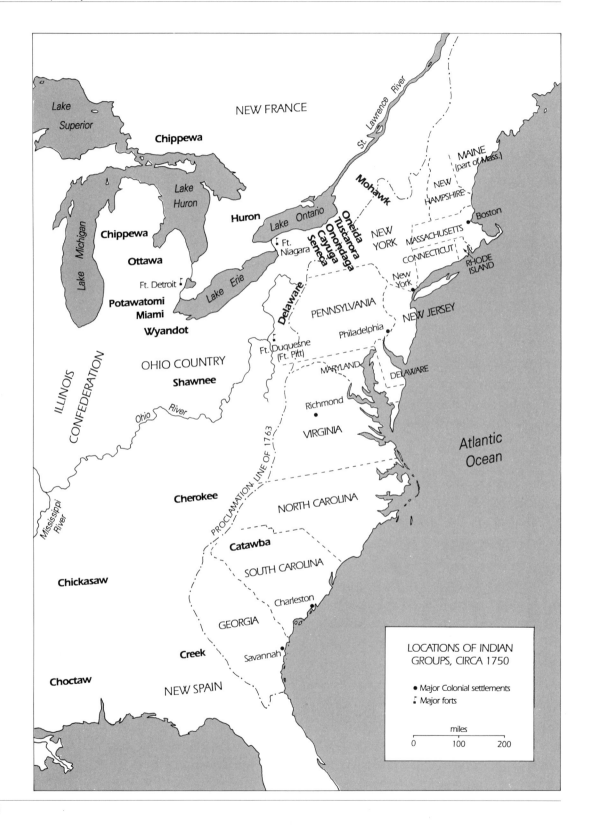

NEW FRANCE

Lake Superior

Chippewa

Lake Huron

Lake Michigan

Chippewa

Ottawa

Ft. Detroit

Potawatomi
Miami

Wyandot

OHIO COUNTRY

ILLINOIS CONFEDERATION

Shawnee

Ohio River

Mississippi River

St. Lawrence River

Huron

Lake Ontario

Ft. Niagara

Lake Erie

Mohawk

Oneida
Tuscarora
Onondaga
Cayuga
Seneca

NEW YORK

MAINE (part of Mass.)

NEW HAMPSHIRE

MASSACHUSETTS

CONNECTICUT

RHODE ISLAND

Boston

New York

Delaware

PENNSYLVANIA

NEW JERSEY

Philadelphia

Ft. Duquesne (Ft. Pitt)

MARYLAND

DELAWARE

Richmond

VIRGINIA

PROCLAMATION LINE OF 1763

Cherokee

NORTH CAROLINA

Atlantic Ocean

Catawba

SOUTH CAROLINA

Chickasaw

Charleston

GEORGIA

Creek

Savannah

Choctaw

NEW SPAIN

LOCATIONS OF INDIAN GROUPS, CIRCA 1750

● Major Colonial settlements

⌐ Major forts

miles

0   100   200

into the forbidden areas. Indian elders knew that traditional ways of life could not long withstand the rising English presence on their lands. For them, the peace after Pontiac's Rebellion spelled defeat. Fearing the changes their children and grandchildren would face in the coming years, they had difficulty feeling joy at the birth of a new generation.

By the 1760s white settlements in the British colonies stretched deep into the continent. A million and a half people populated the Atlantic seaboard, and thousands more migrated to the colonies every year. Between 1760 and 1775 more than 125,000 people fled poor economic prospects in the British Isles and Germany to settle in British America. Adding to this surge in white immigration was the forced migration of at least 85,000 Africans, who were brought to the colonies primarily as agricultural laborers. The transportation of Africans and voluntary immigration of Europeans together resulted in a 10 percent increase in the colonial population in just 15 years. The white population also grew dramatically by natural increase. In the 18th century European women living in America reproduced at a rate previously unknown in human history. Because of the early age at which most women married, the general health of the population, and in many areas the ease of remarriage after the death of a husband, the average white woman gave birth every two to three years. In British America, especially in the colonies north of Virginia, more children lived to adulthood than in Europe at that time. As a result, during the late colonial period, the population doubled approximately every 25 years.

These people needed land, for the majority made their living as farmers. Colonial settlers therefore welcomed the British victory over the French. It meant the opening of vast new areas for settlement. The lands already were inhabited by indigenous peoples, but this fact meant little to the colonists. They regarded Indian culture as barbaric, Indian religious beliefs as contemptible, and Indian use of the land as wasteful. White settlers believed that the Christian God wanted them to occupy the lands of the interior, just as they already had settled the coastal areas.

Such attitudes led European settlers and their families to move steadily onto the lands of the Iroquois in New York, the Delaware in Pennsylvania, and the Cherokee and Catawba in the Carolinas.

They ignored the Proclamation Line of 1763, not only because they had no respect for the rights of the Indians, but also because they disputed the right of the English government to exercise such a vigorous form of control over their lives. When it came to a question of land ownership, English attempts to govern the interior were doomed to failure.

By the time white settlers began to move west of the Appalachian Mountains in large numbers, Native Americans understood their ways well. They knew that the whites would demand exclusive ownership of the lands they farmed, generally fencing in their land to make the point absolutely clear. They also knew that the whites would pay only nominal sums for the areas they claimed and that they would destroy traditional hunting grounds without regard for the Indian way of life. But by the mid-18th century Indians such as the Iroquois of western New York also realized that the white presence would not go away. These people had to be dealt with in one way or another. When open warfare against them did not succeed, the Indians tried diplomacy. On at least two occasions, for example, the Iroquois negotiated peace with the whites by selling off large tracts of land belonging to less powerful Indian dependents. In this way the Shawnee lost their traditional hunting grounds in Kentucky,

An Indian council at Johnson Hall, home of Sir William Johnson, superintendent of Indian affairs.

and the Ohio Valley lands of the Delaware and Mingo were turned over to the whites. Other powerful Native Americans also sometimes sacrificed the interests of weaker tribes in order to maintain some degree of control over white expansion into the interior. By the beginning of the American Revolution in 1775, some interior tribes were completely dispossessed, and others, such as the Seneca, felt severely threatened.

For women as well as men the issues of white expansion and land use were of vital importance. Although Native American men conducted warfare and negotiated treaties and trade agreements, women played important roles in making decisions for peace or war, especially among the powerful Iroquois. They wanted to preserve their traditional way of life as long as possible, and so they supported the efforts of men to control the movements of white settlers.

But for Iroquois women, adjustment to white culture, or acculturation, was less threatening than it was for men. White control over Indian lands meant that Iroquois men could no longer hunt or conduct warfare at will. These were the two aspects of male work that were the most important to the male Native American identity. Women, in contrast, led fairly settled lives, just as the whites did. They farmed, lived in one place most of the year, and concerned themselves with community and family above all else. The major impact of acculturation for Native American women was the sudden necessity to share their traditional work roles of farming and childrearing with men. This transformation required a total redefinition of female and male relationships. The main question loomed: How would women and men change their customary sex roles to make their way of life more like that of the whites who swarmed over Iroquois hunting lands in ever increasing numbers?

The silver medal given by Sir William Johnson to the western Iroquois in 1766. Topped by an Iroquois eagle, it shows an Englishman and Indian shaking hands.

THE COMMUNITY OF WOMEN: CHILDREARING AND THE SEXUAL DIVISION OF LABOR

As the French and Indian War drew to a close, Hannah Breck Parkman of Westborough, Massachusetts, gave birth to her last child, a son named Elias. She and her husband Ebenezer already had nine children, and in addition Ebenezer was the father of four children by his first wife, Mary. The devout wife of a Congregational minister, Hannah undoubtedly viewed her large family with pride. But her health was poor, and the difficulties of providing for so many children were numerous. Families such as hers stretched the resources of farming communities to their limits.

Many years earlier Hannah Parkman's deliveries had begun in tragedy. Only a few months after her marriage in 1737, she suffered a miscarriage. Her first daughter died shortly after birth, and another miscarriage followed a year later. The birth of William in early 1741 signaled the beginning of happier times. In rapid succession Hannah delivered nine healthy children, all born between two and two-and-a-half years of each other. Only Elias's birth was delayed. He arrived almost three years after his older sister Hannah. At the time couples often acted to limit births late in a woman's childbearing years, when her health was more at risk and the family's need for additional children was much reduced.

A mid-18th-century painting by John Greenwood portrays the bond between grandmother and grandchild, both named Abigail Gerrish. Such multigenerational ties were greatly prized in an era when successful reproduction marked the fulfillment of women's highest destiny.

Households such as the Parkmans' were common in the colonies in the mid-18th century. If a woman lived through the rigors of childbirth, she generally conceived again quickly. Aside from abstinence and abortion, effective forms of birth control were unknown. Religious beliefs also made people fatalistic about the problems associated with many pregnancies and births. They thought that God had meant them to have large families. Fertility was viewed as a mark of God's favor, especially when it was accompanied by good health for both a mother and her children. To become a mother and grandmother many times over was to obey God's commandment: "Be fruitful and multiply, and fill the earth and subdue it" (Gen. 1.28).

Women also saw childbirth as a way of atoning for the sin of Eve. According to biblical interpretation of the time, Eve committed the first sin by tempting Adam to eat of the fruit of the Tree of Knowl-

This portrait shows the "stairstep" pattern of birth intervals in colonial families: children spaced about two years apart.

edge. In this way original sin, and the expulsion of Adam and Eve from the Garden of Eden, was regarded as primarily the fault of women. By giving birth, women gained redemption not only for themselves, but for all of humanity. In this way they were thought to be blessed by God. In the 18th-century world, then, American women of European descent earned respect and authority through motherhood.

Large families, however, were difficult to support. Conscientious parents worried about two problems: how to feed and shelter their children properly, and how to prepare them for making their own living when they were grown. By the 1750s a concern of farming families was the scarcity of good farmland. The fact that an entire continent lay before them gave little comfort to people then living on the eastern seaboard. Parents hoped that their children could settle near them rather than move to a frontier area. But land became more and more expensive, and most families could not afford to buy farms in settled areas for all their children. Some sons and daughters had to migrate. Initially, they moved to distant towns and then, as the century progressed, to frontier areas such as Maine, western Massachusetts, New York, Pennsylvania, and even Ohio.

In the South the story was the same. The population there grew more slowly, primarily because the hot climate promoted a variety of lethal diseases, but families still watched with dismay as their children moved away from the home farm or plantation. The Virginian Landon Carter, for example, regretted his daughter Judith's settlement in a distant area after her marriage in 1774. He confided his concerns to his journal while noting the new bride's youthful enthusiasm for her upcoming move:

> Poor Judy and her new sister Sally came here. I could not help observing how easily that poor girl is made to believe her distant happiness when I am certain she sees nothing but misery. She knows not whether she goes up this fall or next spring; I said it might keep her the longer from being miserable for she would be so as soon as she got there; She answered no she should not. I am certain the last time she was here she told me there was no neighbors about the place within 20 miles of it. But possibly it was with her All for Love or the world well Lost.

The rapid rise in the slave population after the mid-18th century made the opening of southern frontier lands essential. Plantations with slave labor forces grew up steadily throughout western

Virginia, the Carolinas, and Georgia.

In the era of the American Revolution (1775–83), most families lived on farms. They raised most of their own food and produced the flax and wool needed to make cloth, and in addition produced some crop or crops to trade. The ideal of the subsistence farm, on which a family raised everything it needed for a comfortable living, rarely was realized. Most people traded crops, goods, and services. Generally, this was accomplished locally, and many individuals never visited the thriving commercial centers of Boston, New York, and Philadelphia. But they came to depend more and more on people who did, traveling peddlers or local merchants who went to large towns and cities to get goods to trade in rural areas. By the mid-1760s urban areas in America had become thriving places to trade, hold court proceedings, and conduct government business. Although

In Edward Hicks's painting of his childhood homestead, his foster mother teaches him to read (bottom right). Colonial mothers typically were in charge of their children's early education.

most people still lived on farms, they depended more and more on commercial areas for necessary services. And the closer a family lived to a trading center, even a small one, the more comfortable it could be. Parents therefore were saddened to see their children settle far from towns and villages.

For women, life on an isolated farm was particularly difficult because of the nature of their work roles and health care needs. Men living in rural areas still traveled to town to conduct necessary business such as selling crops and trading goods produced on the farm. Their work in town gave them opportunities for social interaction, the chance to gossip or discuss the political questions of the day. But women generally stayed close to home, restricted by pregnancy, the needs of nursing infants and small children, and their daily work routines. Even more important was women's need for help during pregnancy and childbirth. Once a woman moved into an area far from her nearest neighbor, she placed herself in a dangerous situation. She could expect little assistance when giving birth, and if she became ill during pregnancy or after childbirth there would be no medical care or household help available. Few women gladly moved away from their relatives, friends, and physicians.

The movement to the frontier, therefore, was regarded by most women as a necessary evil. Many men also saw their isolation as unpleasant and difficult, but on the whole more men than women were challenged and invigorated by the prospect of building a new life on the frontier. The story of the Cumming family was probably typical. After their marriage, the couple moved from Boston to the frontier, where they soon faced danger during the French and Indian War. As a friend reported, "Mrs Cumming is greatly affraid of the French and trys to get Mr Cumming to be willing to move to Boston, but he will not hear nor think any thing about the French, and dont care *two pence* for all the french. They are as safe at York as anywhere, there is no dainger, etc."

Frontier settlers also faced attack and capture by Indian warriors. White women feared living on Indian lands just as much as Native Americans dreaded the settlers' appearance in their territory. If these women could have avoided moving to the dangerous frontier, they would have done so. But with land scarce and the population growing, they saw no other way to make a living and raise a family.

For women on the frontier, life was a series of challenges. Rudely constructed log cabins such as this one exemplified the primitive way of life of settlers.

Many white people drew comfort from their conviction that the Christian God meant for them to live on Indian lands. To the whites, the Indians were wasting huge tracts of valuable farmland. White settlers could not believe that God condoned the Indian way of life. Instead, they were convinced that native inhabitants must be taught the benefits of living as Europeans did. Only when Indians were converted to Christianity and taught to farm did whites feel that the two peoples could live side by side in peace. Colonial leaders, and later, leaders of the new United States, therefore adopted a policy of seizing the vast majority of Indian lands with little or no compensation. They assumed that eventually the indigenous peoples could be acculturated to the ways of white farmers. Then, the leaders believed, Indians would be content with the small parcels of land the whites were willing to leave them.

Until menopause, which generally occurred sometime between

ages 40 and 50, women's adult lives were dominated more by the rhythms of pregnancy, birth, and breast-feeding than by where they lived. Given women's medical needs, midwives and female healers held positions of status and authority. In fact, the only thing approaching a public role available to prerevolutionary women was that of healer or midwife. Women skillful in the use of medicines and knowledgeable about the human body provided valuable services to their neighbors and communities as well as to their own families. They often were as successful as professional physicians in treating their patients. Like many crafts and trades, healing was learned

In this illustration from a 1793 midwifery manual, Man-midwifery dissected, *or* The obstetric family-instructor, *the left side of the figure is a male midwife, the right side a female. Each half holds the tools of the trade. There were many more women midwives than men until after 1780.*

through an apprenticeship. As a result, the daughters of healers and midwives frequently followed in their mothers' footsteps, becoming local experts consulted for their special knowledge and skill. This pattern was just as common for African Americans and Indians as it was for whites.

Although families called on local healers and physicians, they also relied on home remedies to treat the sick. A mother was expected to have at least some medical knowledge. Sarah Pierpont Edwards, wife of the minister Jonathan Edwards, for example, sent medical advice

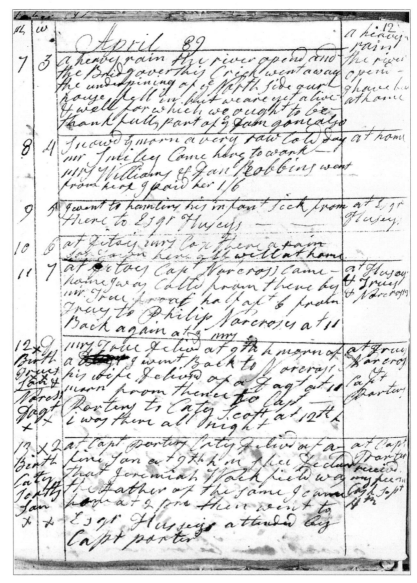

This page is from the diary of Martha Ballard, a midwife in Hallowell, Maine. She delivered 816 babies between 1785 and her death in 1812.

to her daughter in a postscript to one of her husband's letters:

> Your mother would have you use a conserve of Raisons; a Pound
> of good sugar to a Pound of Raisons, after they are ston'd. Mix
> with it, nutmeg, mace, Cinnamon, Cloves, ground in a spicemill,
> with some orange-Pill; one Nutmeg to half a Pound of conserve,
> and the other spices in the same Quantity. Take a little as suits
> your stomach, in the morning, and an Hour before Dinner, and
> in the after-noon.

> . . . Your mother has also an inclination that you should some-
> times try a Tea made of the Leaves of Robins Plantain, If it be
> known at Newark by that name; she says she has found it very
> strengthening and comfortable to her in her weakness.

Jonathan Edwards added his own advice: "I should think it best
pretty much to throw by [avoid] doctors, and be your own Physician, . . . hearkening to them that are used to your Constitution."

Medical knowledge was especially important for rural women
such as Sarah Edwards, who had no physicians or apothecaries living nearby, as urban women did. Literate women often kept medici-
nal recipes, called "receipts," in the same books in which they wrote
down their cooking recipes. A receipt for cough syrup might be found
between recipes for ginger cake and stuffed fowl. In addition, women
grew standard ingredients for medicines in their gardens. Herbs such
as vervain and Jerusalem oak were known to expel worms in children; caraway relieved colic; and marigold quickened the healing of
cuts, bruises, and sprains.

Most women also had experience in attending births. Unlike Native
American women, who generally gave birth alone or with one atten-
dant in an isolated location, white women gathered relatives and
friends together for births in their own homes. Labor and delivery
generally were attended by several female relatives in addition to
the midwife. Hannah Parkman, for example, always was attended
by six or seven women. Gathering the women together was her
husband's job, but he often had the assistance of male friends. When
Elias was born, Ebenezer Parkman reported the event in this way:

> At Eve[nin]g had such Indications of approaching Travail [that]
> N[eighbo]r Batherick being here I desir'd him to call at N[eighbo]r
> Pratts, who is ready to hasten to Granny Mayn[ar]d. wc. [which]
> was done: & Alex[an]d[e]r went to ye Widow Newton, whose
> son bro[ugh]t her Capt[ain] *Wood* went for Mrs Baker who (I

perceive too unwillingly) came—both Mrs. W[illia]mss, Mrs. Pratt
& Mrs. Morse came—all of ym [them] this E[venin]g.

Once the rush of bringing the midwife and neighbors was over,
a husband's work ended. Husbands stayed at hand, but they were
not crucial figures in the birth of their children unless it was not
possible for women attendants to be there. (The modern turnabout
is interesting: Today husbands generally are present at their children's
births, and female relatives and friends are excluded.) Ebenezer, for
example, was not present at any of his children's births. Although
loving, concerned, and even frightened (for he loved his wife dearly),
he remained in the background, visiting Hannah between moments
of crisis but retreating when her pains increased. When Hannah was
in labor with Elias, Ebenezer turned the birth over to more capable
hands and went to bed until, "Ab[ou]t 2 in ye morning Widow Newton
rouses me with the News of a Safe Deliv[eran]ce & ye Birth of a
Son, of extr[aordinar]y Size and Fatness—To God be all Hon[o]r
Praise & Thanksgiving!"

Births were almost public affairs to the community of women.
During a normal labor, women visited, sewed, exchanged bawdy
stories, and gave details of their own past deliveries. Their presence
demonstrated women's concern for each other, the importance of
female bonding at this crucial time, and the significance accorded a
woman's labor—her travail. Friends (Mrs. Baker notwithstanding)
wanted to be at the scene, a part of the ritual of birth. They regarded attendance at a birth as both a duty and a privilege. On a
more practical level, for the new mother the psychological benefits
of having friends nearby was great.

Having at least one nursing mother present at a birth also was
helpful. Midwives sometimes gave laboring women a drink of breast
milk as a way of speeding up contractions. At the time of delivery
the midwife and perhaps one or two other women remained actively
involved, while the others receded to the corners of the room or
went into another room. A friend usually held up the mother as she
gave birth, although in large towns midwives' stools were available
to give her support.

In New England and the middle colonies, where most families
lived in towns, white women rarely delivered alone or with only
their husbands to help them. At worst, married women who lived

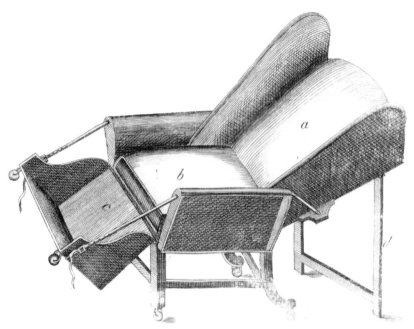

This "Easy chair...useful for lying-in women and sick persons" was shown in a 1793 manual for the care of pregnant women. Birthing chairs, intended to make women in labor comfortable, were generally available only in towns. Rural women made do without them.

nearby could attend, and at best numerous relatives, friends, and a skilled midwife saw a woman through her delivery. This was not so much the case in Virginia and Maryland, where men established their farms up and down the banks of the Chesapeake Bay and all navigable rivers in order to ship their cash crop—usually tobacco—as cheaply as possible. This settlement pattern of isolated farms with few population centers extended into other areas of the South as settlement in the Carolinas and Georgia expanded during the 18th century. The distance between farms meant that there were often few friends or neighbors close enough to attend a birth.

Isolated farm women did everything they could to avoid giving birth alone or with only their husband in attendance. Some women traveled to their parents' homes or asked female relatives who lived far away to visit them to help with their deliveries.

Sometimes even the wealthy delivered without a midwife. Landon Carter was one of the richest men in Virginia, but his daughter-in-law, who lived with him, failed to call for a midwife in time for several of her deliveries. The third time this happened, Carter was furious. The infant was born dead, and after the birth the mother seemed in critical condition. In his diary Carter wrote, "I was just riding out to see the destruction [around his farm after a severe rainstorm] but was called back by my son to his wife then taken in labor the third time without a midwife, so punctual are women or rather obstinate to their false accounts. I found everybody about her in a great fright and she almost in despair. The child was dead and the womb was fallen down and what not." The mother made a complete recovery, but the experience of having no skilled medical care available during a crisis was traumatic for the entire Carter family.

Like their white mistresses, African-American women preferred to have the company of relatives and friends during childbirth. The work routines of slaves often made this impossible, but women other than midwives sometimes were allowed to leave the fields to assist at births. Black and white women regularly attended each other in childbirth, especially when few women lived within easy traveling distance. White women valued the help of a skilled black midwife, and black women similarly relied on the aid of their white mistresses when their labor began. Childbirth was one occasion that called for the breakdown of racial barriers.

Rural women of all ranks assisted each other whenever they could, but at times there was no help nearby. Then a woman and her husband had to do the best they could on their own. For the literate, books were available by the mid-18th century. In fact, one of the

A medical text typical of the sort consulted by colonial American women and their care givers. Sensational images such as this helped make the books best-sellers.

ARISTOTLE's

COMPLEAT

MASTER PIECE.

In THREE PARTS;

Displaying the Secrets of Nature in the Generation of Man.

Regularly digested into Chapters and in Sections, rendering it far more useful and easy than any yet extant.

To which is added, A

TREASURE of HEALTH;

OR, THE

FAMILY PHYSICIAN:

Being Choice and Approved Remedies for all the several Distempers incident to Human Bodies.

The Twenty-Ninth Edition.

LONDON:

Printed and Sold by the Booksellers, 1772.

best-selling books of the period was a manual on sexual matters, pregnancy, and childbirth called *Aristotle's Complete Masterpiece: Displaying the Secrets of Nature in the Generation of Man.* Undoubtedly, many women relied on *Aristotle's Masterpiece* to help them through a lonely, frontier delivery.

Hannah Parkman was fortunate to live in a settled farming area, with neighbors, midwives, and physicians close by, places to trade in town, and Boston only a day's ride to the east. Her residence in central Massachusetts was the colonial ideal: the Parkmans' house was close enough to a major trading area to gain many of its advantages, but far enough away to avoid the threat of disease. Eighteenth-century towns and cities could become life-threatening during epidemics of smallpox, diphtheria, measles, and yellow fever. At such times everyone with the means left town to live with friends or relatives in the country. During the second half of the century, wealthy residents of northern cities often owned country houses or boarded in the country every summer, when diseases swept through large towns, killing hundreds. Rural areas suffered epidemics as well, but disease spread less rapidly and killed fewer people in the country.

The situation south of Pennsylvania was somewhat different. Both country and town were unhealthy in the southern regions, where disease and early death were significantly more common than in the North. Whereas a northern mother might lose only one child out of four before he or she reached the age of 21, a southern mother would lose two. Most southern children saw at least one of their parents die before they reached adulthood, and many children were orphaned. Parental and child death led to relatively unstable family lives in the South. Because of this high death rate and the isolation of the farming population, women in the South had to live more independent lives than those in New England.

Living in a town or city certainly made running a household somewhat easier. Town women who lived above the subsistence level knew conveniences and luxuries that rural women could only dream of—inexpensive cloth imported from England, bakeries, and readily available professional medical care. But even for women in urban areas household management was difficult and time-consuming. Many still had to garden, raise poultry, and tend milk cows. And they also

Living in town made it possible to buy prepared foods such as pies. But as this humorous engraving of a Philadelphia street scene shows, accidents were always a possibility.

raised numerous children while managing their complicated households.

In order to care for their families, neighbors, and relatives, women needed a broad education in both mundane tasks (such as whitewashing the house and raising vegetables) and activities requiring considerable skill (such as caring for the sick and spinning). Many women knew at least a little about healing, producing cloth, dairying, and brewing, and they all performed the day-to-day, backbreaking labor of gardening; preparing and preserving food; raising and killing poultry; hauling water; and in between, of course, bearing, breastfeeding, and caring for their young children. An English folk song, addressed to a newly married groom, mentions one more chore many rural women could not avoid:

> Oats, peas, beans, and barley grow
> Oats, peas, beans, and barley grow

Nor you nor I nor anyone knows
How oats, peas, beans, and barley grow

Now you're married, we wish you joy
First a girl and then a boy
You must be kind, you must be good
And help your wife to chop the wood.

How did women manage to keep up with all their work (including chopping the firewood) and take care of their children, too? They usually had help. In all but the most isolated areas, women labored for each other on a daily basis. The assistance of other women was essential because of a rigidly observed sexual division of labor. Except in rare instances, usually during an illness, men did not do women's work. They faced their own round of daily chores, which were more than enough to keep them busy from morning to dark much of the year. Therefore, the community of women enforced a code of behavior based on the exchange of work and the sharing of their teenage daughters' labor.

Women were most in need of household assistance when their children were young. One infant usually did not prevent a woman from fulfilling her housekeeping obligations, but when a second baby arrived, she needed help. The older child, now usually two to two-and-a-half years old, required constant supervision, and the infant

A woman spins yarn for her family's use. The term spinster *arose from the fact that most spinning was done by unmarried daughters.*

The son corrects the Father, and the Daughter feeds the Mother.

The Wife turns Soldier, & the Husband spinin

In his driving the Miller to Market.

Fishes flying in the Air, & the Sportsman Hunting upon the Water.

In this English print, all the roles are reversed. At top left, the son disciplines his father while the daughter feeds her mother; at top right, a woman takes up arms while her husband does the quintessential female work of spinning.

needed much of its mother's time for breast-feeding. (Bottle feeding was not practiced unless a mother was ill or had died. Lack of sterilization made it unhealthy, and bottle-fed babies rarely lived.) As Esther Edwards Burr, mother of Aaron Burr, observed after the birth of her second child, "[W]hen I had but one Child my hands were tied, but now I am tied hand and foot (how I shall get along when I have got 1/2 dzn or 10 children I cant devise [understand])." During these years women turned to relatives or servants for assistance. If a woman had an unmarried sister or niece, this relative might come to live with her. In the country, neighbors' daughters might act as servants, either on a short-term or long-term basis. In urban areas professional servants could be hired. People of means paid their female servants wages, whereas poorer families relied on exchanges of goods and services.

Enslaved women were not restricted to women's work. White slaveholders did not hesitate to use women as agricultural laborers, although they preferred to purchase male slaves whenever possible. In addition to their agricultural work, however, some slaves helped their white mistresses in the house. Even wealthy women had to labor very hard, and the help of slaves was essential when there were few relatives and neighbors nearby to share work. Enslaved women therefore assisted with both child care and housekeeping, just as white servants did. Acculturated African-American women generally received these jobs because they could speak the language of their owners and had grown accustomed to white customs and manners. As slaves, they were not paid wages, worked long hours, and often were forced to live apart from their own families. Their primary compensation was the opportunity to develop skills valued by whites. On southern farms, baby nurses, healers, midwives, and spinners had a more elevated status than field hands. These skilled workers sometimes received better food, clothing, and medical care.

Despite the expense, most young mothers regarded the help of at least an adolescent girl as a necessity and its absence as an extreme hardship. One young mother complained to her sister about her difficulties in finding help. "I have nobody with me nor have had since Commencement, tho' throu mercy I have my helth as well

Slave women were responsible for agricultural chores as well as for minding their own children and the master's, as depicted in this 1854 print.

as ever I had in my life or I could not possibly get a long in any shape. But you know there is nobody to have. *Girls* are very scarce for all are *Ladys* now a days." Because of the demand for their labor, adolescent girls were considered vital members of their communities. Their status is suggested by one rural minister's diary entry for March 17, 1756: "Betty Bellows dyed about 10 am., age 18 years. Extremely sorrowful in that House and Neighbourhood, there being no other daughter in that Family, and but one or two more young Women in that Corner of ye Town." The help of young women, both in their own families and the families of neighbors, was so important that this man could sense the sorrow of an entire neighborhood at the death of so useful a member.

Inadequate household help was not only inconvenient or burdensome for a mother. It could actually prove to be dangerous for young children, who consequently went without adequate supervision. While a housewife tended the fire or milked her cows, a youngster might pull over a kettle of boiling water, pick up a knife carelessly left within reach, or wander away into the fields or the woods. Esther Burr described one such accident involving a toddler who was visiting her in 1755: "About six weeks ago she fell into the fire and burnt her hands and face most tirrably, but is like to recover with the loss of one of her fingers."

In the spring of 1756 Ebenezer Parkman attended the funeral of a neighbor's child who "dyed by means of being burnt by a Warming pan." As he noted, the death could easily have happened in his own family. Only the previous fall one of his sons had narrowly escaped drowning. Parkman wrote, "Little John Sav'd from Drowning. Bill had dug a Hole in Neighbor Barnabas Newtons meadow in Time of Drought, which was now fill'd with Water; into this John fell and Samuel pull'd him out." John was barely two years old; Samuel recently had turned four.

In the absence of adequate child care, mothers sometimes relied on physical restraints to control the movements of their very young children. A high chair or go-cart, the colonial equivalent of a modern baby's walker, could keep a child from crawling underfoot or into an open fireplace. But such devices could not replace a mother's watchful eye, and accidents still occurred. One journalist thanked God for the "memorable deliverance of my little Hannah. The Cel-

A colonial go-cart in action, in an illustration from a children's book of the period. Such go-carts helped restrain children's movements while their mothers worked at spinning and other household chores.

lar Door was left open, & she in her Go Cart pitch'd down, & went to ye bottom—yet without any gr[ea]t Hurt."

Throughout the 19th century women's household chores became less difficult and time-consuming as a result of industrialization and the transportation revolution, which allowed the inexpensive movement of goods to rural areas. Formerly overworked and therefore somewhat neglectful mothers could then focus more energy on caring for their infants and young children. As a consequence, families became more child-oriented and the importance of the mother-child bond increased.

One example of this shift in attitudes can be seen in the use of go-carts. In the early 19th century, Mary Hunt Tayler, an influential writer on child care, criticized the devices. Referring to go-carts as "pernicious inventions," she wrote that they "are rapidly growing obsolete... and I sincerely hope they will ere long be consigned to complete oblivion, together with scull caps, forehead cloths, swaddling bands and stays, in which our great grandmamas used to imprison their hapless offspring." Cruel or not, "imprisonment," of course, was the purpose of these restraints. Without it, more children would have been injured, and more mothers made frantic by the antics of their offspring.

When a family's oldest child reached the age of seven or eight, household help became less critical. Even young children helped their mothers in numerous ways, but especially with child care. Given the sexual division of labor, girls were particularly useful as mothers' helpers, which explains why the English folk song "Oats, Peas, Beans, and Barley" expresses the hope that a newly married couple's first-born would be a daughter. Apparently, most people thought that women needed help in the house even more than men needed it in the fields or the shop.

Despite the many claims on their time, most white women were able to work in or near their own houses, where they could keep an eye on their children while laboring at other chores. Black field-workers and the poorest white farm wives, however, had to take their infants and toddlers into the fields with them. Just like Iroquois women, many women of African descent came from a tradition in which women were the agricultural workers. They would have observed traditional customs of child care when more than one woman shared the work. If a farm had enough laborers—and in the South this was more and more often the case as the 18th century progressed—an elderly woman might be placed in charge of caring for

White plantation owners evaluate the merchandise at a slave auction, including a mother and child. Families were often separated at auction.

several very young children while their parents worked. On larger farms and plantations slave women might be allowed to return home to breast-feed their infants at certain times during the day, or a baby might be brought to its mother for nursing. In either case, from a very early age black children had to learn to be independent of their mothers for most of the day. Only on Sundays were women allowed to spend all of their time with their children. If they attempted to subvert the slave system by demanding more time for their children, they might be punished. One planter described a long-standing dispute with his female slaves over their breast-feeding schedules:

> I discovered this day what I never knew before, nay what I had positively forbid years ago, but negroes have the impudence of the devil. Last year the suckling wenches told the overseer that I allowed them to go in five times about that business; for which I had some of them whipt and reduced it to half an hour before they went to work, half an hour before their breakfast; and half an hour before they go in at night. And Now they have made the simpletons believe I allow them to eat their morning's bit. So that a wench goes out to bake for that, then they must have their time to eat it, then another bakes for their breakfast. But these things I have forbid upon their Peril.

Whites interfered with slave mothers' care for their children in many ways, but by far the greatest threat facing these women was the possibility that their offspring might be sold. Under the law any child born of a slave mother also was a slave, and therefore could be sold at any time. Slave marriages had no legal validity, which gave slaveowners the right to separate slave spouses at will. As a result, enslaved women lived with the constant fear that they might be separated from their children and husbands. When an owner migrated to a new area, suffered financial setbacks, or died, black workers went up for sale. Most owners made no attempt to keep families together. As a rule, only breast-feeding infants were sure to stay with their mothers, for otherwise the babies were likely to die. Their death would rob their white owners of valuable property.

Slave women also lived with the knowledge that they could not control their children's play, work, explorations about the farm or plantation, or interaction with whites. When stingy owners did not give slaves adequate allowances, they even had difficulty feeding and clothing their children. Slave women and men supplemented their allowances by raising vegetables and poultry, but their only time to work for themselves was at the end of the day and on Sundays. The difficulties and heartache of raising children to be slaves led some women to resist childbearing by practicing abortion. But most women just did the best they could to care for their children under slavery. The alternatives—running away, engaging in violent resistance, or committing suicide—would have left their children even more vulnerable to the slave system.

The second half of the 18th century witnessed a subtle improvement in the conditions of slavery for some American blacks. More and more farms developed large slave work forces, thereby giving slaves a greater chance to interact and create close, and therefore protective, family ties. Previously, most farms were so small that their owners could afford to buy only one or at most a few slaves. Developing tight bonds with family members was then far more difficult for transported Africans and even African Americans.

Large plantations were made possible by a rapid increase in slave importations during the decades just preceding the Revolution. The shock of capture, sale, and the trans-Atlantic voyage for individuals must have made any meager improvements in the slave system as a whole seem unimportant. In addition, newly transported Africans were handicapped by language barriers and cultural differences, for they had followed many different ways of life in their own homelands. Therefore, the slaves born in the colonies profited most from living on the expanding plantations. Throughout this period they developed a distinctive African-American culture, which gave them both comfort and strength in dealing with the trauma of life under white domination.

The changes that came with the growth of plantations and economic diversification benefited enslaved men more than enslaved women. Historians have shown that improved farming methods in the Chesapeake produced a new sexual division of labor. In the 17th and early 18th centuries tobacco and corn, virtually the only crops planted, were produced using primitive farming techniques. Workers of both sexes labored side by side at most agricultural chores. For example, both women and men hoed, weeded, spread manure, and cleaned out swamps. As the 18th century progressed, more planters shifted to growing wheat or other grains and to raising livestock.

Men then received new and valued work assignments. Plowing, which became necessary when wheat replaced tobacco as a cash crop, was defined exclusively as a man's job because it required greater strength than hoeing. Cutting lumber, fishing, milling, shearing sheep, and sowing and mowing grains used as fodder for livestock also demanded at least some degree of skill. They all became defined as men's work. Artisan work, such as coopering (making wooden casks), shoemaking, and smithing, also was performed by men, and as the economy grew more labor of this kind was needed. Meanwhile, women continued to work at their traditional unskilled jobs. The new women's jobs that came with greater economic diversification included cleaning winnowed grain, shelling corn, breaking up newly opened fields by hand, and cleaning stables. These tasks were the most monotonous and distasteful.

Another important distinction between men's and women's labor under slavery concerned the way in which it was performed. As

Slave families built their own African-style huts on the grounds of Southern plantations. Mulberry Plantation in South Carolina, shown here, grew indigo and rice.

George and Martha Washington derived great wealth from the use of slave labor, as this image of Mount Vernon, their estate, reveals.

unskilled laborers, women more often than men worked in gangs, under the close eye of an overseer or gang leader. Thus they had little freedom to determine the pace of their work and the order in which assignments were completed. Men also tended to perform a greater variety of tasks than women, thereby reducing the monotony of their work.

According to the plantation records of George Washington, work suitable for men was distinguished carefully from work suitable for women. Washington grouped his male slaves together into one labor force and placed women in a separate group that also included adolescent workers of both sexes. The men's jobs included plowing, harrowing, sowing, cutting timber, carting goods, and making ditches and roads. Men often worked alone and could vary their tasks from day to day. Women were responsible for weeding fields, erecting fences, cleaning stables, spreading manure, harvesting and husking corn, and many other laborious and unpleasant chores. Unlike men, women worked at the same chores day after day until they were completed, rarely or never labored alone, and usually came under the supervision of an overseer. Men therefore came to be seen as the more skillful workers, a distinction that must have affected women's and men's attitudes toward their work and perhaps their private relations as well.

The white men who dominated 18th-century southern society assigned few slave women to either artisan or domestic work. Some women became artisans, particularly spinners or weavers, but they were exceptions. And most southern households, even relatively prosperous ones, got by with little domestic help. Wives and daughters of plantation owners were expected to do most of the gardening, cooking, cleaning, and sewing.

Plantation owners neglected these traditional areas of women's work because they did not value them. Whereas white women might have welcomed the help of enslaved women in the dairy or garden, white men preferred to keep their female slaves busy in the fields. They did not care if their tables lacked butter or fresh vegetables. Content with whatever their wives and daughters might produce, plantation owners in essence were denying the importance of traditional women's domestic labor. Thus both black and white women lived in a culture that devalued their work, while demanding that they labor intensively from sunup to sundown. For enslaved women this harsh work life was devoid of creative labor, with little chance of completing one task from beginning to end. Burdened by both race and sex, the lot of these workers was the worst of all.

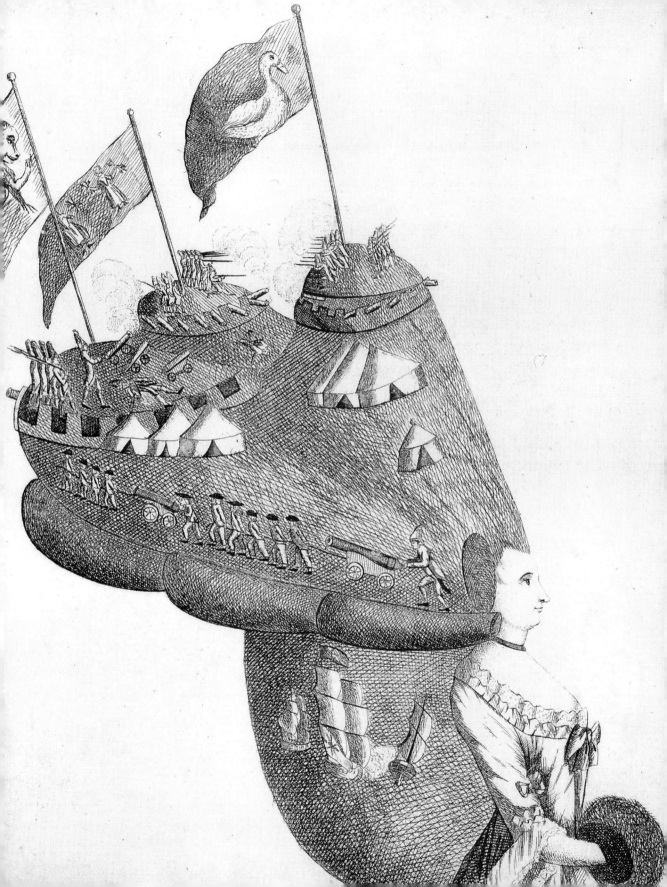

CHAPTER 3

AN ERA OF CHALLENGES: WAR AND THE PROSPECT OF INDEPENDENCE

Women's lives in early America frequently were disrupted by warfare. The colonial period witnessed many wars, some between European powers and others between Europeans and Native Americans. Women participated in all of these wars, although only in rare instances did they actually engage in hand-to-hand combat. Instead, they provided food, shelter, nursing, and other assistance when fighting occurred near their homes or while traveling with an army as camp followers. With their husbands they paid taxes to support the troops. They were captured and held as prisoners for exchange or sale. When men were drafted for military service, they left their wives in exclusive charge of both children and family businesses, which required an unusual level of energy, fortitude, and independent initiative. Most colonial women were more accustomed to playing the part of helpmate than head of the family.

During the American Revolution, women once again met the challenges presented to them. But this war differed from previous conflicts. It demanded that women and men make new kinds of political decisions. In the years leading up to the war, women were forced to confront ideas about the nature of government and their roles in it. Whereas previous wars were almost exclusively territo-

This 1776 British engraving, entitled Bunkers Hill, or America's Head Dress, *lampoons the meager battle plan of the British generals Howe and Gage. Portraying their defensive mounds in the midst of an absurd woman's hairstyle was considered the ultimate insult.*

rial disputes, this one focused on the proper relationship between a government and the governed. For the first time people in America had to think about the advantages and disadvantages of living under a representative democracy and take a position either supporting or rejecting the idea of independence. Not surprisingly, different women came to different conclusions. Some were avid patriots; others were equally adamant about their loyalty to the British Crown. Still others, particularly members of the Society of Friends (also known as Quakers), were pacifists, people philosophically opposed to all wars.

Serious conflict between the American colonists and England began shortly after the end of the French and Indian War (1754–63). England had gone deeply into debt to pay for the war, and government leaders approved a series of tax measures meant to raise money in America to help reduce that debt. The new laws were opposed by many colonists, who were accustomed to paying taxes only at the local and colony level. Americans did not oppose paying England customs duties, and giving the mother country control over trade, for that was part of a mutually beneficial trading relationship between England and her colonies. But they did not want to become subject to the English Parliament in other ways. In particular, they did not welcome taxation by a governing body that cared more for the interests of the mother country than their own. Being part of the great British Empire gave the colonists many economic advantages, but those might all be lost if Parliament began to oppress them through burdensome taxes.

Fear of financial oppression at the hands of a distant government was one of the major causes of the American Revolution. But there were also other causes. Americans feared losing their liberties as well as their money. The issue of taxation demonstrated that they were not in complete control of their own lives. They had no elected representatives in Parliament and therefore possessed no way of controlling English legislation. English leaders enacted many regulations the colonists hated, such as the Proclamation Line of 1763. In addition, they removed the colonists' right to trial by jury in certain kinds of legal cases and denied them the right to print paper money. The English also disallowed laws enacted in America that conflicted with English laws, including the right to divorce, which many colonists supported but the English Parliament opposed. All of these actions threatened colonial autonomy, and people feared what might come next. But even more than the specific laws enacted by Parliament, many of the colonists resisted what those laws stood for in general: control by a distant, increasingly alien government.

The colonists had not always perceived England as an alien nation with interests different from their own. Throughout the colonial period relations between the mother country and her colonies had been cooperative and mutually beneficial. This was in large part because England had left the colonists alone. Self-government was customary, and it served both groups of people well. But after the

The Pennsylvania Journal *published this reply to the Stamp Act in 1765, using a skull and crossbones in place of a British government seal in the stamp at top right.*

The TIMES are Dreadful Doleful Dismal Dolurous, and DOLLAR-LESS.

of the STAMP

An Emblem of the Effects of the STAMP O! the fatal Stamp

Adieu Adieu to the LIBERTY of the PRESS.

Thursday, October 31. 1765.

THE

NUMB 1195

PENNSYLVANIA JOURNAL;
AND
WEEKLY ADVERTISER.

EXPIRING: In Hopes of a Resurrection to LIFE again.

I am sorry to be obliged to acquaint my readers that as the Stamp Act is feared to be obligatory upon us after the *first of November* ensuing (The Fatal To-morrow), The publisher of this paper, unable to bear the Burthen, has thought it expedient to stop awhile, in order to deliberate, whether any methods can be found to elude the chains forged for us, and escape the insupportable slavery, which it is hoped, from the last representation now made against that act, may be effected. Mean while I must earnestly Request every individual of my Subscribers, many of whom have been long behind Hand, that they would immediately discharge their respective Arrears, that I may be able, not only to support myself during the Interval, but be better prepared to proceed again with this Paper whenever an opening for that purpose appears, which I hope will be soon.

WILLIAM BRADFORD.

French and Indian War, England increased her demands on the colonies. English leaders wanted a tighter relationship in which the colonists would increase the wealth of England not only through trade but through direct taxation as well. And they opposed Americans' attempts to legislate in ways different from their own.

Issues such as these were not considered women's concerns in the mid-18th century. Social customs dictated that women defer to men in many areas of life, and one of these was politics. Undoubtedly, many women formed and voiced opinions about local political questions—where to locate a bridge or whether a school should be built, for example. But women felt less comfortable expressing their opinions on broad questions about the nature of government and the rights of the governed. The primary reason was the difference in the intellectual training of women and men. Only men were expected to read and study the great political thinkers of the day, to understand their arguments and consider their shortcomings. Because women rarely received an advanced education, they were made to feel inferior intellectually. As a rule, women's opinions were not respected, even when they possessed the training necessary to develop them.

Many men of ordinary social rank felt just as uncomfortable expressing political ideas as women did. More men than women were literate at all social ranks in colonial America, but most still had only a basic education. They could read and write and keep accounts, but they did not spend their evenings reading political philosophy. They might read the local newspaper occasionally but little else. Unless they believed their lives were threatened in some direct way, ordinary workingmen did not trouble themselves with politics. They left political decision making to their social betters, just as women did. The fact that only men of property were allowed to vote in local and colony-wide elections prevented many men in the lower ranks of society from feeling they had a right to express political opinions. The same attitudes prevailed among women of all social ranks, for even the wealthiest women could not vote in early America.

When England began to tax the colonists after the French and Indian War, poor men and women as well as the elite felt the effects of the new policies. Although they might not have understood the implications of English legislation in all areas, they did recognize when they were being asked to shoulder a new financial burden. And they did not like it. While elite men debated the place of the colonies in the British Empire, ordinary men and women focused on the simple question of whether or not they would pay the new taxes. And as it turned out, virtually all Americans agreed that the taxes

An engraving by Paul Revere shows British troops, sent to force the colonists to pay British taxes, entering Boston Harbor in 1768.

A VIEW OF PART OF THE TOWN OF BOSTON IN NEW ENGLAND

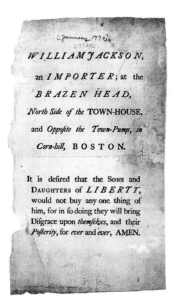

The patriotic Daughters of Liberty were active participants in boycotts against tea and other luxury items forbidden by the Townshend Acts.

were oppressive and should not be submitted to without a fight.

Between 1764 and 1776 the colonists strongly opposed English taxation policies. In these years women came to feel that they had not only a right but also a responsibility to form and express political opinions. Men, who at first felt uncomfortable discussing politics with the women in their families, came to see that if women were asked to support a war, they had to understand and believe in the cause for which they were fighting. Many years passed before the colonists achieved the consensus necessary to declare independence from Great Britain, years filled with debates about the nature of government and the rights of the governed. Women participated in those debates alongside men.

To protest English taxes, American commercial and political leaders signed agreements of nonimportation and nonconsumption. Merchants made pacts not to import English goods, and citizens agreed not to consume them. In order to make these agreements effective, most people had to participate in them, and women's contribution was important. Women not only had to refrain from purchasing imported items they usually bought, such as tea, but also had to increase their production of homemade goods. By refusing to drink tea, a staple of their diet before the Revolution, colonial women showed their commitment to the Patriot cause. Similarly, Loyalist woman drank tea to show their support for a continued close relationship between England and the colonies.

An important way in which women and teenage girls expressed their opposition to English policies was through participation in spinning bees. Gathering on the town common or at a minister's home, teenagers and young women would set up their spinning wheels and work together all day. Their goal was the production of homespun—cloth that was made in America rather than imported from England. By participating in a spinning bee, and by working long hours at home spinning, weaving, knitting, and sewing, American women were helping to make the colonies independent of English goods. Public rituals such as spinning bees helped them understand the significance of their work. Most of the spinners at these occasions were unmarried. Married women were too busy with their babies and household chores to spin or weave. They left this work to adolescent girls and unmarried women—the spinsters of the age.

In this 1775 British engraving, entitled "Society of Patriotic Ladies," women in North Carolina draft a pledge not to drink tea. Behind them, other women empty their tea containers. The unflattering appearance and behavior of the women indicated English disapproval of such unfeminine political activity.

The significance of women's home production also was demonstrated by the appearance in public of prominent men and women dressed in homespun clothes. Wearing homespun would have been considered a sacrifice, for it was rough and unattractive compared to cloth imported from England. One year the entire graduating class of Harvard College attended commencement dressed in homespun. Political leaders of the revolutionary cause wore homespun for many public appearances. And many individuals, women and men, wore homespun as a way of demonstrating their support for the colonial

Anna Green Winslow of Boston was one of many young women who participated in the resistance to the British. Like many young girls of her time, she was well informed and concerned about political matters.

government. As 13-year-old Anna Green Winslow put it in her journal in the winter of 1771, "As I am (as we say) a daughter of liberty, I chuse to wear as much of our own manufactory as possible." The efforts of girls like Anna were necessary to make the nonimportation agreements of colonial governments workable.

Direct and personal accounts of spinning bees are rare, but a variety of sources such as newspaper reports can create a picture of a typical bee. The following is a story of what one girl's experience might have been:

The young woman sat quietly beside her father on the seat of the wagon, glancing back to check on her spinning wheel whenever they jounced over potholes in the well worn road leading to town. She was excited and a little nervous, but her natural temperament was mild and so she just sat silently, thinking of the day ahead, not chatting with her father as other girls might have done. In fact, she was like her father in this regard. They both preferred action to words, and showed their thoughts by what they did rather than what they said. Today the daughter would show her opposition to the English Parliament by spinning in a public spinning bee held at the minister's home. The thread she produced could be woven into homespun cloth, a useful commodity now that the colonists were intent on reducing their dependence on imported English goods.

The wagon lurched as it came to a stop. Father and daughter jumped down to lift the heavy spinning wheel to the ground. They set it off to the side of the house, in a less conspicuous location than some others were choosing. While the young woman wanted to do her share to fight the hated taxes, she did not like being the center of attention. Proper women knew their place, and it was not in front of crowds. She would have preferred the quiet of her family's sitting room to the glare of the sun at the minister's house. But father said these public displays were important for teaching people their duty, and she had agreed to come for his sake. He was giving so much of his own time and money to oppose the new taxes. As a member of the local Sons of Liberty, it was his duty to make sure local shopkeepers and tavern keepers were observing the nonimportation agreements. His own store had suffered in trade since the agreements were signed, for now all his English goods were stacked in the back of the shop. He could not sell them, although he had paid for them with his own credit before the confrontation with England began. She had to help him. Fortunately, there were more and more wagons coming down the road. Many wheels would turn today, for the cause of liberty.

Fifty spinning wheels whirled and clicked through the morning. The girls and women worked hard, for at the end of the day they would see who had spun the most. Here was an opportunity to show industry and skill at the wheel, which were both valued traits in wives. At midday the wheels stopped and for a moment, an unnatural quiet settled on the crowd. The spinners were tired and hungry. Then a fiddle picked up and the laughing and talking began. They gathered around tables filled with local produce and piled their plates with the simple, homegrown fare. There were no teas imported from the Far East for this crowd. They drank herbal tea and coffee. This was one of their greatest sacrifices, for the colonists loved their im-

American women had always spun yarn, but during the Revolution their boycott of the British textile industry and willingness to produce more homespun cloth became crucial to the war effort.

*ported teas. More than one person felt the effects of an upset stom-
ach after drinking strong coffee that day.*

*By late afternoon the wheels turned slowly. The women's arms
and backs ached with the efforts of the day. The town's minister
rang the signal bell to stop the spinners, and as they joined their
families he began his sermon in honor of the occasion. He praised
the spinners for their work, calling them "Daughters of Liberty,"
and applauded the seriousness with which they, their families, and
neighbors had treated the occasion. By showing their support for
nonimportation, they had struck a blow for freedom and advanced
the patriot cause. He concluded his words of praise and thanksgiving with a rousing call for further acts of female patriotism: "Yes,
Ladies, you have it in your power more than all your committees
and Congresses, to strike the Stroke, and make the Hills and Plains
of America clap their hands." By making homespun and giving up
tea and other imported goods, they could show the British "that
American patriotism extends even to the Fair Sex, and discourage
any future Attempts to enslave us." His words pleased the listeners,
who seldom received much praise for the domestic chores they worked
at day after day. Before and during the Revolution, the need for
home production made women's work seem more important than it
usually did.*

After participating in a public ritual such as a spinning bee, girls
and women could not help but have political thoughts and feelings.
They said that after working all day they "felt Nationly," a new
sentiment for many. Other women developed political opinions in
response to different influences. In towns and cities, for example,
women shopkeepers who might otherwise have wished to remain
outside the fray were forced to decide whether they supported colonial resistance efforts. They were visited by local committees that
made sure no one was selling imported English goods. With their
activities scrutinized and their business reduced, the shopkeepers had
to decide for themselves whether American resistance was necessary
or foolish. In short, the colonists' efforts to persuade Parliament not
to tax them aroused the female as well as the male population. It
was virtually impossible not to form an opinion, and social customs
dictating female silence on political questions went by the wayside.

As Sarah Franklin wrote to her father, Benjamin Franklin, in the fall of 1765 (during the period of opposition to the taxes on legal documents, newspapers, and other goods imposed by the Stamp Act), "Nothing else is talked of. The Dutch talk of the stomp ack, the Negroes of the tamp. In short, everybody has something to say."

In the end most Americans resisted English taxes. Acceptance of a declaration of independence was another thing, however. Many Americans could not make the leap from tax resistance to military support for independence. Only after a full decade of agitation did leaders of the resistance effort convince the colonists that independence from England was the one way to guarantee their liberties. Even after the outbreak of war, the Loyalist minority was powerful. The group was composed of many leading citizens, men and women whose business, religious, and political ties to England made the prospect of independence unattractive. An estimated one-fifth of the colonists remained actively opposed to the Revolution throughout the war; another two-fifths were neutral. This neutral group showed a tendency to support whichever forces were winning, siding in particular with the troops that controlled their local communities. Basically, they just wanted to be left alone. Some neutrals, among them many Quakers, were pacifists. They opposed all warfare, particularly over issues such as taxation. Only about two-fifths of the population gave active support to the Patriot cause. With the neutrality or opposition of so many citizens, George Washington had a hard time forming and maintaining an army. That was one reason that the war lasted so long, more than six years.

For black Americans the choices were just as confusing and difficult as they were for whites. They were unsure which side, if any, they should support. The Patriots talked in glowing terms of freedom from slavery, but they meant freedom from their own enslavement to British tax officers rather than an end to the labor system that forced tens of thousands of Africans and African Americans into bondage. The British seemed to offer the best opportunity for enslaved people to improve their lives. In an attempt to undermine the Patriot cause, British commanders promised freedom to all slaves who joined the Royal Army. The offer applied to women and children as well as men, for the British were just as interested in preventing colonial farmers from maintaining a work force as they were

Sarah Franklin Bache, the daughter of American diplomat Benjamin Franklin, was a member of the Philadelphia Ladies Association, which went door to door to raise money for shirts for revolutionary soldiers.

in increasing the army's size. As a result, thousands of Africans and African Americans refused to join the revolutionary cause and sided with the Crown. Whenever the British army came near them, they abandoned their farms and plantations. These people fled from lives without hope, turning to the only available option for freedom.

The Sawyer family of Norfolk, Virginia, was one slave family that was determined to take the risks involved in escaping to the British lines. Living separately under three different owners, the mother, the father, and three children must have thought the British offer was their one chance to be together. In 1776 they made it to British-held territory. What they found there could only have terrified them. With inadequate food, shelter, and medical care, hundreds of escaped slaves were sick and dying from smallpox. Most of them would die that winter before they had the chance to begin a new life of any kind. The Sawyers were lucky. They were all still alive in 1782, when the British included them on a list of people deserving the continued protection of the Crown after the English surrender to the Americans.

Epidemic disease was a continual threat in all army camps, and one of the gravest problems for blacks who joined the British. Another serious difficulty was managing to escape with children. Women more often than men fled from slavery with children in tow, largely because fathers were so often separated from their families under the slave system. During mothers' escapes, babies and toddlers had to be carried, fed, and kept quiet. Young children had to be encouraged to be brave and uncomplaining as they traveled long distances with little food. When they finally reached British lines, women with children were faced with still more challenges. Children were more susceptible to disease than adults, so mothers had to struggle just to keep their offspring alive. And in addition to caring for their children, the women had to perform the work assigned to them by the British army.

The difficulties slave women faced in traveling with children explain why relatively few of them had attempted to escape from slavery before the Revolution. Until the English offered protection, there was no safe haven nearby. For women accompanied by small children, even a distance of a few miles could be an impossible obstacle to freedom. In their escapes, men and the few women who joined them traveled hundreds of miles to unknown areas. Some joined

Indian communities; others traveled to distant colonies or Canada, usually on foot. All endured tremendous privations. Recapture was common, and stiff physical punishment the norm. Because it was virtually impossible to escape with children along, most women chose to remain where they were, enslaved but allowed to live with their daughters and sons.

After the English made their offer of protection, however, mothers suddenly saw that escape was possible. Thousands risked suffering, sickness, even death to win freedom for themselves and their children. Their bravery as they hid from their pursuers and comforted their frightened children cannot be overestimated. Ironically, the same force that drove them into the arms of the British—freedom—also compelled their masters and mistresses to join the revolutionary cause.

The onset of war forced white women to face other types of hardships and challenges. Twenty-year-old Jemima Condict of Pleasantdale, New Jersey, recorded in her journal her thoughts and fears as the conflict began. In the fall of 1774 she wrote, "It seams

At the Battle of Lexington on April 19, 1775, Major Pitcairn (on horseback) leads the British troops. The engraving was made by a Connecticut militiaman, Amos Doolittle, from drawings done by artist Ralph Earle on the scene.

we have troublesome times a Coming for there is great Disturbance a Broad in the earth & they say it is tea that caused it. So then if they will Quarel about such a trifling thing as that What must we expect But war & I think or at least fear it will be so." Six months later her fears were realized. She then wrote:

> Monday Wich was Called Training Day I Rode with my Dear father Down to see them train, there being Several Companys met together . . . How soon they will be Calld forth to the feild of war we Cannot tell, for by What we Can hear the Quarels are not like to be made up Without bloodshed. I have jest Now heard Say that All hopes of Conciliation Betwen Briten & her Colonies are at an end for Both the king & his Parliment have announced our Destruction. fleet and armies are Prepareing with utmost diligence for that Purpose.

The war began in Massachusetts on April 19, 1775, with the battles of Lexington and Concord. Word spread quickly throughout the colonies. Jemima Condict wrote of the first bloodshed of the war shortly after it occurred: "As every Day Brings New Troubels So this Day Brings News that yesterday very early in the morning They Began to fight at Boston, the regulers [British soldiers] We hear Shot first there." Jemima probably heard as well of the Battle of Bunker Hill, which took place near Boston on June 17. The British suffered their largest casualties of the war in that battle—more than 800 wounded and 228 killed.

After that, the two armies had no more major engagements for a year. Both sides dug in and waited. Then the British decided to leave New England, which they saw as the region of the colonies most hostile to their cause. In June 1776 they moved their army to New York, not far from Jemima Condict's home. Soon she was writing of the deaths of her neighbors' sons: "We hear News from our army . . . & Several of them we hear is Dead. Sense there Departure Benjamin Canfeild & Stevan Morris, David Luis Died with the Camp Disorder & william acorn we hear was killed by the injins; Jabez freman, the Son of the Late Deceast John freman is Dead, Also Sias Heady Died up there with Sickness."

New Jersey women and men suffered tremendous hardships in the fall and winter of 1776–77. Failing in its attempt to defend New York City, the American army abandoned the city in late summer. Washington and his troops then retreated across New Jersey, with the British in pursuit. Unable to make a firm stand against the invaders, Washington's forces surrendered town after town. The English, and their hired German troops, known as Hessians, plundered and looted throughout the colony. Rape was common, as was the murder of unarmed civilians, including women and children. In this dark season, the Patriot cause seemed close to defeat. One woman, a Quaker named Margaret Morris, decided to remain in her home in Burlington, New Jersey, even though the British troops were approaching and many of her neighbors and friends were choosing to flee. Her journal, which she kept throughout the winter and spring of 1776–77, is a rich account of a woman's life in occupied territory during the war.

On December 7, 1776, Morris wrote, "A letter from my next neighbors Husband at the Camp, warnd her to be gone in haste, and many persons coming into Town today, brought intelligence that the British Army were advancing toward us." Morris, a widow, decided to remain in her house and trust in God to protect her. Her sister, who lived with her, agreed. As devout Quakers, the women had faith that God would not let the innocent suffer with the guilty. Although they never met with any personal injury that winter, they frequently feared for their lives. On the night of December 11, when "a large body of Hessians" arrived in Burlington, they hid in their cellar until the firing of cannons and muskets stopped. They learned the next day that Patriot troops had almost fired at their house. The troops thought that the light burning there meant Hessian soldiers were inside.

Women living close to the lines of battle had many opportunities to act bravely in the face of danger. Accounts of women serving as spies, carrying messages across enemy lines, and hiding men from their enemies were common throughout the war. Margaret Morris was one such courageous figure. A few days after the near attack on her house, American soldiers searched it for a Loyalist sympathizer, who was, in fact, hiding in a secret room. Morris's quick actions saved her friend from discovery. She reported the encounter later:

> A loud knocking at my door brought me to it. I was a little fluttered & kept locking and unlocking that I might get my ruffled face a little composed, at last I opend it, & half a dozen Men, all Armd, demanded the keys of the empty House [next door]. I asked

Margaret Hill Morris, a Quaker pacifist living in Burlington, New Jersey, helped both Loyalists and Patriots during the British occupation of her town. Her journal is a rich source of information about the revolutionary era.

what they wanted there they said to search for a D—d tory who had been spy[in]g at them from the Mill.

Morris was relieved that the soldiers believed the Tory was hiding at her neighbor's house and not in her own. She warned her friend of his danger by pulling a string attached to a bell in his hiding place: "I rung the bell violently, the Signal agreed on, if they came to Search." Then Morris played the fool to further mislead the search party:

> "I put on a very simple look & cryd out, bless me, I hope you are not Hessians—say, good Men, are you the Hessians?"
> "Do we look like Hessians?" asked one of them rudely.
> "Indeed I dont know."
> "Did you never see a Hessian?"
> "No never in my life But they *are Men,* & you are Men, and may be Hessians for any thing I know—but Ill go with you into Col[onel] Co[xe's] house."

She proudly concluded her story: "So I marchd at the head of them, opend the door, & searchd every place but we could not find the tory—strange where he could be." That night she went into Burlington with her "refugee," as she called him, and found him safer quarters. On the way home she seized an opportunity to do another good deed: "I was told to day of a design to seize on the person of a Young Man in town, as he was deemed a tory. I thought a hint w[oul]d be kindly rec[eive]d and as I came back calld on a fr[ien]d of his, & told him—next day he was out of . . . reach."

Quakers such as Margaret Morris often sympathized with the Loyalists. They thought the Patriot call to arms was sinful and unnecessary. Yet many Quakers, Morris among them, clearly supported the efforts of their revolutionary neighbors as well. Morris referred to Washington's army as "hers," and provided food and shelter to hungry Patriots whenever she could. After Washington defeated the British at the Battle of Trenton on December 26, 1776, American soldiers landed at Morris's wharf and spent the night in her neighbor's empty house, which she took care of. One man later wrote in his journal, "The good woman next Door Sent us 2 Mince pies Last Night, which I took very kind."

A few days later, when other soldiers had stopped to sleep in the house, she visited them to tend the fires and mourned for their suffering: "About bed time I went in the next house to see if the fires were safe, & my heart was melted with Compassion to see such a number of my fellow Creatures lying like Swine on the floor fast aSleep, & many of them without even a Blanket to cover them." As a mother, Morris's heart went out not only to the young men, but also to their mothers, who did not know the suffering of their children. When the soldiers left, she wrote pensively in her journal, "Several of *my* Soldiers left the next house, & returnd to the place from whence they came . . . There were several pritty innocent looking lads among them, & I simpathized with thier Mothers when I saw them preparing to return to the Army."

Later that spring Morris was called on to perform another service for the military. Like many other women during the war, she used her knowledge of medicine and healing to help the sick. Several Patriot boatmen and their wives were ill and needed medical attention, but no doctor was available. As a skilled healer, Morris kept medicines at hand to give to the poor. Her reputation in town caused them to turn to her for help, but she hesitated to leave her

A British cartoon of 1775 illustrates the difficulties that American soldiers' wives and children experienced during the war.

house. "They Ventured to come to me—& in a very humble manner begd me to come and do something for them—At first I thought they might have a design to put a trick upon me & get me aboard of thier Gondolas—& then pillage my house, as they had done some others." But after discovering that the sick people were lodging in the governor's house, which she considered safe, Morris went to see them. She correctly diagnosed their illness as "the itch fever," and treated them so that they all recovered. "They Thankfully acknowledged my kindness," she wrote.

Morris's experiences were common for women who lived near the scenes of battle. When asked, local women performed many services for the soldiers on both sides. But the armies did not depend only, or even predominantly, on local residents for provisions and medical care. Many women traveled with the troops and worked for wages as cooks, laundresses, and nurses. They were known as camp followers, and are remembered, unfortunately, more for the sexual services they provided than for any others. But the soldiers relied on the food they prepared, the wounds they dressed, and the shirts they washed. Camp followers provided an important and necessary labor force for the armies. Continually short of manpower, Washington's army depended heavily on its womanpower to take care of the day-to-day needs of the soldiers.

Some women, especially those with no children and no independent means of support, became camp followers by accompanying their husbands into service. Traveling with the army, they could share their husbands' lives and offer them extra care and encouragement. They also were fed by the army, a significant consideration for many of these poor women. Others were escaped slaves or free blacks looking for a way to support themselves during the war. Still others *were* prostitutes or became prostitutes to earn money after they began working for the army.

A few women rejected traditional female roles during the war and took on men's jobs. Women such as Mary Hays McCauley were not content to remain behind the lines during a battle. She earned the nickname Molly Pitcher because she carried water to thirsty soldiers on the front lines. On June 28, 1778, at the Battle of Monmouth, New Jersey, Molly's husband fell, either because he was wounded or merely overcome by the fatigue of the battle. Molly then assumed his place and loaded a cannon until the end of the engagement. Her bravery later earned her an annuity, an annual payment, from the federal government.

The winter of 1776–77 marked one of the lowest points of the war for the Patriot cause. General Washington had not yet proved himself an able commander, and the British were sending more and more troops to the colonies. On the assumption that a strong show of force would frighten the colonists into submission, England was dispatching a larger number of men to America than it had ever before sent overseas. The English had never fought a war like this

This woodcut of a woman holding a musket was printed in "A New Touch on the Times...By a Daughter of Liberty," published in Massachusetts in 1779. The identity of the woman is not known, but her firm posture reveals her determination to aid the Patriot cause.

Deborah Sampson dressed as a man to serve in the revolutionary army and received regular rations and pay. After the war she supported herself by giving lectures about her experiences.

one and had underestimated the difficulties of subduing a population spread over a vast territory. Even though many colonists openly or tacitly supported England in the war, not all chose to fight on the side of the British armies. The Loyalists gave England little actual help, and the Patriots were a fiercely driven minority.

The Patriots' determination became clear after the English easily entered and gained control over Philadelphia, Pennsylvania, in the late summer of 1777. Philadelphia was the capital of the fledgling United States and a port of strategic importance. The city was also filled with Loyalist sympathizers and neutrals because of its large Quaker population. But despite the English victory there, the people in the countryside refused to surrender. Washington's army had lost the city, but had defended it well in two engagements. And a major American victory at Saratoga, New York, in mid-October gave the Patriot cause new strength. In that battle more than 6,000 Loyalist soldiers had been forced to lay down their arms.

When France entered the war on the side of the Americans in February 1778, Washington and his advisers became even more confident of their ability to win. The English might have captured major ports, such as New York and Philadelphia, but they could not control the countryside. The Americans suspected that these outlying areas were where the Revolution would be won.

The loss at Saratoga and stiff resistance in Philadelphia caused English commanders to reassess their overall strategy. They decided to shift the main focus of the fighting to the South. The English believed there were many more Loyalists or neutrals in the southern colonies than in the North, which meant the southern population would be easier to subdue. In fact, more southerners *did* have mixed feelings about the war. Many slaveholders feared losing their workers to the British. Even worse, they feared slave revolts. In Georgia the number of blacks equaled the number of whites. In South Carolina the majority (more than 60 percent) of the population was black. Support for the Revolution was noticeably cooler in these colonies than it was in New England or the middle colonies.

The first southern engagements of the war in 1779 convinced the English that they were right. Savannah and Augusta, two of Georgia's major cities, fell easily. The British then committed a large force to the defeat of Charleston, South Carolina, which fell in May

1780. General Benjamin Lincoln, the leader of the Americans in Charleston, was forced to surrender his entire army of 5,500 men along with the city. As English troops fanned out over the country-side, hopes faded. Many previously neutral people joined the invaders, convinced that they would be the ultimate winners.

Faced with these disasters, the Patriots held firm. Instead of giving up, they dedicated themselves to the war effort with renewed energy. One sign that the Patriot cause was alive and well was an intercolonial effort by women to raise money for the troops. Not since the Revolution's early days, when the Daughters of Liberty held their spinning bees, had women organized in support of independence. Although many women made sacrifices throughout the war, they did so individually.

After the fall of Charleston, a group of elite women in Philadelphia led by Esther DeBerdt Reed, wife of Joseph Reed, the governor of Pennsylvania, decided that a major, unified effort was necessary to encourage the troops. They formed a committee to go door-to-door in the city to ask the women and girls of each household to contribute money for the soldiers. The committee suggested that women with large or medium-sized incomes go without luxuries, such as

A British cartoonist tried to discourage revolutionary colonists with this frightening cartoon (1779), blaming General Washington for the ragged state of the nation. The artist urged colonists to view the cartoon "as if in a mirror."

fancy hairstyles and jewelry, and give equivalent money to the cause. Poorer women were asked to contribute whatever they could. No one was overlooked.

To prepare the city's inhabitants for the collection, Reed wrote an article titled "Sentiments of an American Woman." It said that American women should express their gratitude to the troops for their tremendous personal sacrifice in defending the colonies. Fending off potential criticism of her committee's efforts as unfeminine, she noted that many women in the past had acted heroically for their people and their countries and received praise for doing so. Joan of Arc was her favorite example, but she also cited Old Testament figures, female monarchs, and Roman matrons. She then argued that opposition to the women's relief effort would be unpatriotic. Her defensiveness and the care with which she justified the women's work before they had even begun shows that this effort was an unprecedented activity for women.

Philadelphia women collected a large sum for the troops in the early summer of 1780. They then expanded their efforts, writing to friends and relatives in other areas encouraging their participation in the fund-raising campaign. Esther Reed's "Sentiments" was published in newspapers throughout the colonies in July. In response, women in other colonies set about organizing their own committees. When all the money was collected, Reed wrote to General Washington informing him of the women's gift. His grateful reply included a request that the money be used to make shirts, because the troops were poorly clothed and winter was approaching. If the women made the shirts themselves, Washington noted, the army could save additional money by avoiding the cost of hiring seamstresses.

Reed was disappointed by this suggestion. She wanted to give the men something special, a monetary supplement to the pay they were receiving from the government. She did not want the women's gift to become a substitute for clothing the troops already should have been given for their services. Reed wrote to Washington, "Soldiers woud not be so much gratified by bestowing an article to which they look upon themselves entitled from the public as in some other method which woud convey more fully the Idea of a reward for past Services & an incitement to future Duty." She proposed that instead of shirts, money be delivered directly into the hands of the men. She wanted

THE SENTIMENTS of an
AMERICAN WOMAN.

ON the commencement of actual war, the Women of America manifested a firm refolution to contribute as much as could depend on them, to the deliverance of their country. Animated by the pureft patriotifm, they are fenfible of forrow at this day, in not offering more than barren wifhes for the fuccefs of fo glorious a Revolution. They afpire to render themfelves more really ufeful; and this fentiment is univerfal from the north to the fouth of the Thirteen United States. Our ambition is kindled by the fame of thofe heroines of antiquity, who have rendered their fex illuftrious, and have proved to the univerfe, that, if the weaknefs of our Conftitution, if opinion and manners did not forbid us to march to glory by the fame paths as the Men, we fhould at leaft equal, and fometimes furpafs them in our love for the public good. I glory in all that which my fex has done great and commendable. I call to mind with enthufiafm and with admiration, all thofe acts of courage, of conftancy and patriotifm, which hiftory has tranfmitted to us: The people favoured by Heaven, preferved from deftruction by the virtues, the zeal and the refolution of Deborah, of Judith, of Efther! The fortitude of the mother of the Macchabees, in giving up her fons to die before her eyes: Rome faved from the fury of a victorious enemy by the efforts of Volumnia, and other Roman Ladies: So many famous fieges where the Women have been feen forgetting the weaknefs of their fex, building new walls, digging trenches with their feeble hands, furnifhing arms to their defenders, they themfelves darting the miffile weapons on the enemy, refigning the ornaments of their apparel, and their fortune, to fill the public treafury, and to haften the deliverance of their country; burying themfelves under its ruins; throwing themfelves into the flames rather than fubmit to the difgrace of humiliation before a proud enemy.

Born for liberty, difdaining to bear the irons of a tyrannic Government, we affociate ourfelves to the grandeur of thofe Sovereigns, cherifhed and revered, who have held with fo much fplendour the fcepter of the greateft States, The Batildas, the Elizabeths, the Maries, the Catharines, who have extended the empire of liberty, and contented to reign by fweetnefs and juftice, have broken the chains of flavery, forged by tyrants in the times of ignorance and barbarity. The Spanifh Women, do they not make, at this moment, the moft patriotic facrifices, to encreafe the means of victory in the hands of their Sovereign. He is a friend to the French Nation. They are our allies. We call to mind, doubly interefted, that it was a French Maid who kindled up amongft her fellow-citizens, the flame of patriotifm buried under long misfortunes: It was the Maid of Orleans who drove from the kingdom of France the anceftors of thofe fame Britifh, whofe odious yoke we have juft fhaken off; and whom it is neceffary that we drive from this Continent.

But I muft limit myfelf to the recollection of this fmall number of atchievements. Who knows if perfons difpofed to cenfure, and fometimes too feverely with regard to us, may not difapprove our appearing acquainted even with the actions of which our fex boafts? We are at leaft certain, that he cannot be a good citizen who will not applaud our efforts for the relief of the armies which defend our lives, our poffeffions, our liberty? The fituation of our foldiery has been reprefented to me; the evils infeparable from war, and the firm and generous fpirit which has enabled them to fupport thefe. But it has been faid, that they may apprehend, that, in the courfe of a long war, the view of their diftreffes may be loft, and their fervices be forgotten. Forgotten! never; I can anfwer in the name of all my fex. Brave Americans, your difintereftednefs, your courage, and your conftancy will always be dear to America, as long as fhe fhall preferve her virtue.

We know that at a diftance from the theatre of war, if we enjoy any tranquility, it is the fruit of your watchings, your labours, your dangers. If I live happy in the midft of my family; if my hufband cultivates his field, and reaps his harveft in peace; if, furrounded with my children, I myfelf nourifh the youngeft, and prefs it to my bofom, without being affraid of feeing myfelf feparated from it, by a ferocious enemy; if the houfe in which we dwell; if our barns, our orchards are fafe at the prefent time from the hands of thofe incendiaries, it is to you that we owe it. And fhall we hefitate to evidence to you our gratitude? Shall we hefitate to wear a cloathing more fimple; hair dreffed lefs elegant, while at the price of this fmall privation, we fhall deferve your benedictions. Who, amongft us, will not renounce with the higheft pleafure, thofe vain ornaments, when fhe fhall confider that the valiant defenders of America will be able to draw fome advantage from the money which fhe may have laid out in thefe; that they will be better defended from the rigours of the feafons, that after their painful toils, they will receive fome extraordinary and unexpected relief; that thefe prefents will perhaps be valued by them at a greater price, when they will have it in their power to fay: *This is the offering of the Ladies.* The time is arrived to difplay the fame fentiments which animated us at the beginning of the Revolution, when we renounced the ufe of teas, however agreeable to our tafte, rather than receive them from our perfecutors; when we made it appear to them that we placed former neceffaries in the rank of fuperfluities, when our liberty was interefted; when our republican and laborious hands fpun the flax, prepared the linen intended for the ufe of our foldiers; when exiles and fugitives we fupported with courage all the evils which are the concomitants of war. Let us not lofe a moment; let us be engaged to offer the homage of our gratitude at the altar of military valour, and you, our brave deliverers, while mercenary flaves combat to caufe you to fhare with them, the irons with which they are loaded, receive with a free hand our offering, the pureft which can be prefented to your virtue,

By An AMERICAN WOMAN.

Esther DeBerdt Reed, shown here in a portrait by Charles Willson Peale, was the wife of Pennsylvania governor Joseph Reed. In 1780 she penned a broadside called "The Sentiments of an American Woman," in which she praised Patriot troops and called on her fellow citizens to contribute money to relieve their poverty.

each soldier to receive two dollars in hard currency, rather than the depreciated continental paper money they usually received as pay.

Washington rejected Reed's proposal. He insisted that the women make shirts. To give the soldiers hard currency would only encourage their dissatisfaction with what the government could provide. "A taste of hard money," he wrote, "may be productive of much discontent as we have none but depreciated paper for their pay." In addition, he feared that some men would spend the money foolishly on drink.

Although disappointed that she could not do something more directly beneficial for the soldiers, Esther Reed accepted Washington's

Mercy Otis Warren, playwright, historian, and close friend of Abigail Adams, in a portrait by John Singleton Copley. Warren hosted revolutionary political meetings in her Plymouth, Massachusetts, home and later wrote a controversial history of the Revolution.

suggestion and organized the production of the shirts. Tragically, she died of dysentery before her work was completed, but others took it up. In late December 1780 thousands of shirts, each embroidered with the name of the woman who had made it, were sent to the quartermaster general in Philadelphia. Praising the women for their patriotism, Washington offered his thanks on behalf of the troops. He assured the women that his men would appreciate the shirts and bless them for their efforts.

The women's original goal—raising funds—was untraditional. Yet ultimately they were forced back into a traditional female role, that of seamstress. Washington probably believed that the money would be best used for shirts, but he ignored the sentiments of the women involved when he asked them to make the clothing. The women wanted to do much more. In the end, however, they did achieve something greater than just sewing for the army. They created the Ladies Association, the first intercolonial women's organization in North America. Before the Revolution there was no such thing as a women's club. Even church or maternal associations were unheard of. By organizing to provide active support for a cause they believed in, these women learned the value of working together. They also demonstrated to themselves and to men that they could perform tasks traditionally defined as men's work. The Ladies Association, therefore, taught the new nation something important about women's interests, values, and goals. Just like men, Patriot women could express their political beliefs through their actions. After the war some women remembered the lessons they had learned and founded women's organizations to serve other ends. And they did not forget the political lesson that activism was required to meet the challenges of the age.

Despite the Patriots' best efforts, the campaigns of 1780 went badly for the American cause. The British did well in the early southern campaigns, as thousands of white Loyalists and escaping black slaves came to their assistance. But although the British could capture territory, they could not defend it. Bands of marauding Patriots kept the British from establishing firm control over rural areas.

In the winter and spring of 1780–81 American armies were successful in a number of engagements. They defeated the British first at Kings Mountain and then at Cowpens, both near the border be-

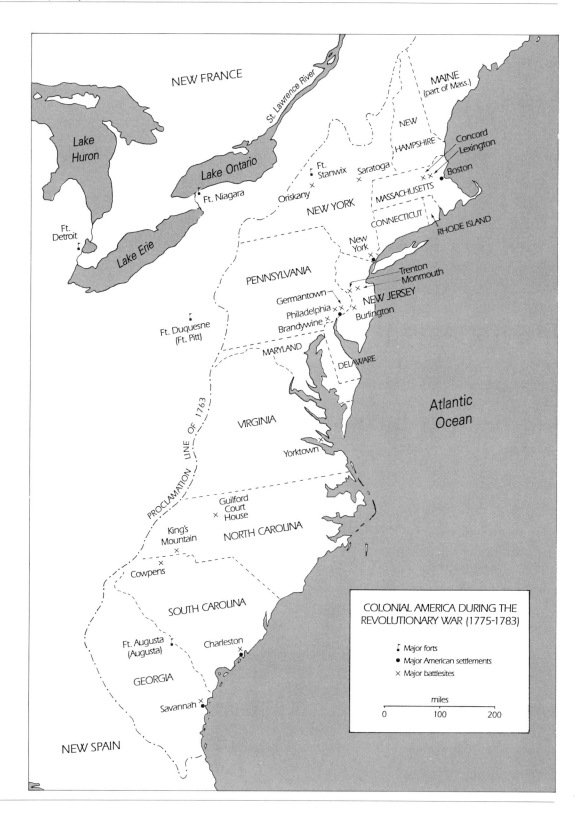

NEW FRANCE

Lake Huron

Lake Ontario

St. Lawrence River

MAINE (part of Mass.)

NEW HAMPSHIRE

Ft. Stanwix

Saratoga

Concord
Lexington

Boston

Ft. Niagara

Oriskany ×

NEW YORK

MASSACHUSETTS

CONNECTICUT

RHODE ISLAND

Ft. Detroit

Lake Erie

PENNSYLVANIA

New York

Trenton
Monmouth

Germantown

NEW JERSEY

Philadelphia × ×

Burlington

Ft. Duquesne
(Ft. Pitt)

Brandywine ×

MARYLAND

DELAWARE

Atlantic
Ocean

PROCLAMATION LINE OF 1763

VIRGINIA

Yorktown

Guilford
Court
× House

King's
Mountain ×

NORTH CAROLINA

× Cowpens

SOUTH CAROLINA

Ft. Augusta
(Augusta)

Charleston ×

GEORGIA

Savannah ×

NEW SPAIN

COLONIAL AMERICA DURING THE
REVOLUTIONARY WAR (1775-1783)

⌐ Major forts
● Major American settlements
× Major battlesites

miles

0   100   200

tween North and South Carolina. At Guilford Court House, North Carolina, General Nathanael Greene decimated the main English army under Charles Cornwallis in March 1781. Then, as Cornwallis moved his troops north into Virginia, he made a disastrous mistake. Stationing his large force of 7,200 men on a peninsula between the York and James rivers, he left the army vulnerable to attack from both land and sea. Washington recognized his foe's error and quickly moved the largest body of his troops from New York to Virginia. As a French fleet attacked the English vessels sent to rescue Cornwallis, Washington trapped the English general. Cornwallis surrendered his army on October 19, 1781. This battle was the last major engagement between the British and the Americans. In response to Cornwallis's humiliating defeat, the English Parliament voted to cease military operations. Independence had been won.

The Comte de Rochambeau, commander of the French troops who supported the revolutionary cause, accepts the surrender of the British at the Battle of Yorktown in October 1781. General George Washington (on horseback, just left of the American flag) observes the ceremony.

CHAPTER 4

INDEPENDENCE REALIZED: NEW DIRECTIONS FOR AMERICAN WOMEN

The Treaty of Paris, which ended the American Revolution, gave Americans an unusual opportunity in modern history: the chance to create a republican form of government. At the time only two nations—Switzerland and Holland—were republics. Hereditary positions in governing bodies (such as the House of Lords in the English Parliament) were common in Europe. They gave certain families the automatic right to govern. Many people believed that large and populous nations needed the kind of discipline that monarchs could impose. The United States, therefore, was embarking on untried ground as it readied itself for republican rule.

Political theorists at the end of the 18th century taught that republics were fragile. Their survival depended on a homogeneous population that believed in honesty, frugality, and sacrifice for the common good. Citizens of a republic had to be both personally virtuous and dedicated to preserving high moral values in their leaders. Honorable and intelligent men needed to elect leaders who could rule dispassionately, with an eye to promoting the welfare of the country as a whole. Narrow self-interest had no place in a republic. Leaders had to be willing to make political compromises, because continual disagreements on basic issues could rip a republic apart.

The first issue of the Lady's Magazine and Repository of Entertaining Knowledge *(1792), published in Philadelphia, combines American patriotic stars with classical imagery to represent republican women. In an allusion to* A Vindication of the Rights of Women, *a radical but widely read book by the British writer Mary Wollstonecraft, a woman presents a petition called "The Rights of Woman" to the figure of Liberty.*

These requirements were particularly important to a republic as geographically large and as ethnically and culturally diverse as the new United States.

People all over the world asked themselves: Are the citizens of the United States virtuous enough to be citizens of a republic? Is there enough honor in the souls of the voters to prevent them from

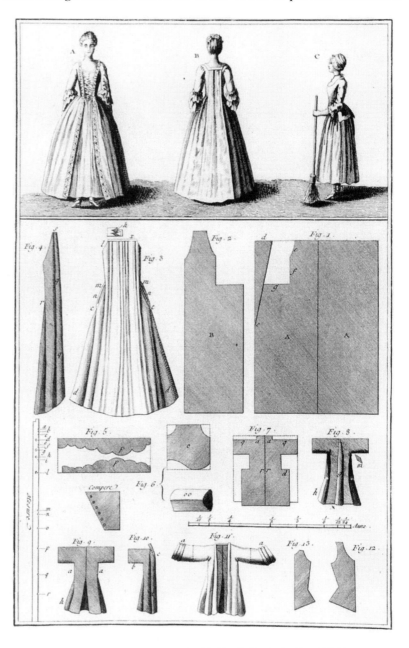

This French fashion plate of 1777 served as a model for American dressmakers after the war. Such books supplied detailed patterns as well as finished drawings of European styles.

accepting bribes? Are they intelligent enough, and respectful enough, to choose the right representatives? Although many leaders of the Revolution believed Americans were extremely virtuous, they could not be sure their new system of government would work. Danger signs were all around them.

Following the war, Americans quickly returned to prerevolutionary standards of dress and consumption. After years of sacrifice for the revolutionary cause, people in the middle and upper ranks of society once again wanted to display their wealth and good taste. Gone was homespun; on display were imported silks and satins. Even more disturbing was the fact that common working men and farmers, who lacked the advantages of higher education, were being elected to high government offices. Some people worried that they did not have the proper intellectual background for leadership roles at this critical time.

One response to concern over the capabilities of voters was widespread improvement in public education. Rather than concluding that representative democracy was too risky an experiment (the position of Loyalists and many neutrals as well), supporters of the United States worked to improve the intellectual capacity of the average citizen. Soon after the Revolution, voters in northern states first called for the use of tax money to finance public schools. In 1789 Massachusetts became the first state to require towns to provide free elementary education to all children. The South could not immediately imitate this and other progressive developments. Devastated by years of British occupation during the war, southerners concentrated on reestablishing their economy. But elsewhere, in the middle and northern areas of the country, more and more free schools opened their doors. "The Spirit for Academy making is vigorous," wrote Congregational minister Ezra Stiles in 1786. He had witnessed the opening of 12 new academies in Connecticut in just five years.

Republican leaders also acted to improve the educational environment of the nation in other ways. Before the American Revolution, education was viewed by most people as a means of promoting the personal well-being of their children, not the well-being of society as a whole. As a result, more sons than daughters were educated, and to a higher level. Most people considered higher education unsuitable for girls, believing it would make them unfit for their duties as wives and mothers. As one man, a Harvard graduate, put it, "Girls

Abigail Adams sat for this portrait in London while her husband was serving as the new United States' first minister to England. An avid correspondent, she regretted her own inadequate education and often apologized for her spelling and grammatical errors.

knew quite enough if they could make a shirt and a pudding." The Connecticut poet John Trumbull expressed his feelings in verse:

> And why should girls be learned or wise,
> Books only serve to spoil their eyes.
> The studious eye but faintly twinkles
> And reading paves the way to wrinkles.

Colonial parents were also concerned about the expense of educating daughters, because most teachers then were hired privately.

Many people thought girls needed to read so that they could study the Bible and later instruct their own children at a basic level. Writing, however, was considered a frill, and arithmetic was taught only to a privileged few girls. "I regret the trifling narrow contracted Education of the Females of my own country," wrote Abigail Adams to her husband John in 1778. "You need not be told how much female Education is neglected, nor how fashionable it has been to ridicule Female learning."

Similar attitudes affected the education provided for boys at the lower ranks of society. Their future work as farmers, clerks, or laborers did not require higher learning. Most people thought that common working men needed only basic literacy and some facility with numbers so they could keep accounts. These assumptions changed with the establishment of a republic. Now, in addition to rudimentary reading, writing, and arithmetic, schools sought to teach children to think independently, reason, and express their opinions clearly and forcefully. According to Thomas Jefferson, even primary schools should be designed to "instruct the mass of our citizens in these their rights, interests and duties, as men and citizens." Now history, rhetoric, and oratory—subjects that previously had been taught only to boys headed for college—were included in the basic curriculum for all students in public schools.

For the first time independent thinking also became a desirable characteristic in women. The instruction of girls was not meant to prepare them to take part in political life. Women were not citizens on a par with men in the new United States. Except in New Jersey, they could not vote or hold public office. In most ways the establishment of a republic had left women's political status unchanged. But in a few important if subtle areas, progress was made. Women's work as mothers assumed greater political importance. Mothers were

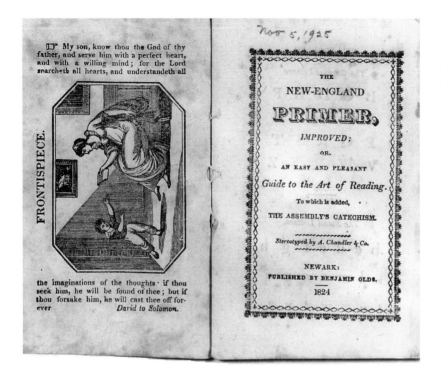

The New-England Primer *was one of the texts used by American women to teach their children to read. It drew its examples from the Bible.*

largely responsible for the early education of their children. They could rear either strong, virtuous children who would become valuable citizens or lazy, ignorant youngsters who would be corrupted easily and thus become undesirable members of society. Because of this influence, much of the future of the nation was seen as resting with its mothers. As one young woman explained:

> A woman who is skilled in every useful art, who practices every domestic virtue . . . may, by her precept and example, inspire her brothers, her husband, or her sons, with such a love of virtue, such just ideas of the true value of civil liberty . . . that future heroes and statesmen, when arrived at the summit of military or political fame, shall exaltingly declare, it is to my mother I owe this elevation.

Women's work as mothers was considered most important in the rearing of sons, who would participate directly in the political life of the republic. But even women without sons received recognition. Virtuous women were thought to influence all the men around them. Acting the part of good citizens would be easier for husbands, brothers, and fathers if they received the support of their female relatives.

Illustrations of female clothing were intended to make arithmetic books entertaining for young American girls. but math was a low priority in most girls' education.

Physician Benjamin Rush of Philadelphia was an active supporter of women's higher education. He wanted them to be well versed in serious academic subjects so that they could raise their sons to be intelligent and virtuous citizens.

For women to do their job properly, they needed to possess high moral standards. They could learn these standards best if they were educated and religious. Ideally, all women should be able to read, write, keep accounts, and think logically about current issues. They were also expected to attend church and heed the moral directions of their ministers.

The middle and upper ranks of American society had even higher standards for women's education by the end of the 18th century. Among wealthy women, poor reading, writing, and speaking skills became socially unacceptable. Elite men wanted their daughters to receive an education similar to that of their college-bound sons. At the same time, young men came to value educated young women as marriage partners. They wanted their wives to be capable not only of raising their children properly, but also of conversing intelligently about the topics of the day. As Benjamin Rush, a Philadelphia physician noted for his efforts to improve female education, explained, "One cause of the misery of many families, as well as communities, may be sought for in the *mediocrity* of knowledge of the women. They should know more . . . in order to be happy themselves, and to communicate happiness to others."

In response to this demand, educators in the major urban areas of the Northeast opened female academies, which were roughly the equivalent of high schools today. Their founding was a major breakthrough for women's education. The curriculum of female academies focused a great deal of attention on subjects previously considered frills: rhetoric, grammar, geography, history, arithmetic, and oratory. Now the areas of study that once had been thought essential for elite women—music, dancing, and needlework—were regarded as recreational activities or not taught at all. Although many girls continued to study these subjects and to receive praise for doing so, intellectual development was regarded as equally or more important.

One of the earliest and most successful female academies was the Philadelphia Young Ladies' Academy. Most of its students were from local families, but some came from as far away as Maine, South Carolina, and the West Indies. They lived with relatives or friends in the city and attended the school by day. For the first time, girls from elite families regularly left home to attend school. Before the Revo-

lution wealthy men occasionally had sent their daughters abroad to study and learn the highest social graces, but the behavior of these fathers was considered almost eccentric. Now, sending a daughter to a female academy became an important way for a family to demonstrate its social standing and good taste.

Soon boarding schools for girls also opened. They appeared in rural areas as well as towns and answered a need for families who did not have relatives living in a northeastern city. One of the most successful was the Moravian Seminary in Bethlehem, Pennsylvania, which had a reputation for strictly supervising the morals of its students while providing an advanced curriculum. As one mother, Elizabeth Chester, reported to an acquaintance, "The people of the society appear very amiable in their manners; and honest simplicity, void of affectation characterizes them.... As to the morals of a child, the Parent may repose entire confidence in the directors, who pay the strictest attention to check every deviation from delicacy & decorum."

This intricate needlework image created by 12-year-old Rachel Thaxter reveals an atmosphere of wealth and decorum. The work was probably done while she attended the Derby Academy in Hingham, Massachusetts, in 1796.

Parents were particularly concerned that their daughters receive moral instruction at boarding schools, where girls lived for extended periods of time. At the Moravian Seminary, for example, students stayed for a maximum of about three years, beginning when they were as young as 10 to 12 years old. Chester was also careful to note, "The [school] government is a government of persuasion, calculated more to attach the affections than pain the body." Her comment indicates that the teachers did not punish the students by striking them, a common method of managing unruly schoolboys during this period.

Letters between young scholars and their parents reveal that the girls understood the importance of their new educational opportunities but also missed the comforts and emotional support of home. Fourteen-year-old Eliza Southgate, away from home for the first time, wrote of her new experiences:

The Moravian Seminary at Bethlehem, Pennsylvania, about 1786. Here, girls received close supervision while they boarded away from home. This was one of the earliest female boarding schools.

Medford May 12, 1797

Honored Parents:

   With pleasure I sit down to the best of parents to inform them of my situation, as doubtless they are anxious to hear,—permit me to tell them something of my foolish heart. When I first came here I gave myself up to reflection, but not pleasing reflections. When Mr. Boyd [her brother-in-law] left me I burst into tears and instead of trying to calm my feelings I tried to feel worse. I begin to feel happier and will soon gather up all my Philosophy and think of the duty that now attends me, to think that here I may drink freely of the fountain of knowledge, but I will not dwell any longer on this subject. I am not doing anything but writing, reading, and cyphering. There is a French Master coming next Monday, and he will teach French and Dancing. William Boyd and Mr. Wyman advise me to learn French, yet if I do at all I wish you to write me very soon what you think best. . . Mr. Wyman says I must learn Geometry before Geography, and that I better not begin till I have got through my Cyphering.

   We get up early in the morning and make our beds and sweep the chamber, it is a chamber about as large as our kitchen chamber, and a little better finished. There's 4 beds in the chamber, and two persons in each bed, we have chocolate for breakfast and supper.

   Your affectionate Daughter

ELIZA SOUTHGATE

When mothers wrote to their daughters at school, they frequently stressed the importance of diligence and urged their daughters not to waste their time. In turn, many girls recognized that they had been given a privilege their mothers had not enjoyed, and that their absence from home represented considerable maternal sacrifice. After all, during these years they could be of greatest help to their mothers in running their households. For some families, doing without a teenage daughter's labor must have been as difficult as paying the cost of her higher education. With this in mind, Eliza wrote apologetically to her mother when she learned that her younger siblings were ill:

Medford, Aug. 14, 1797

Dear Mother:

   I am very sorry for your trouble, and sympathize with you in it. I now regret being from home, more than ever, for I think I might be of service to you now the children are sick. I hope they will be as much favored in their sickness now, as they were when they had the measles. I am very sorry that Jane has broken her arm, for it generally causes a long confinement, and I fear she has not got patience enough to bear it without a great deal of trouble. I suppose that Isabella will be very much worried about her babe. I would thank you to write me very often now—for I shall be very anxious about the children.

I am your affectionate and dutiful daughter

ELIZA SOUTHGATE

Although Eliza regretted her yearlong absence from home, she also enjoyed the intellectual atmosphere of school. At times her work gained precedence over her family obligations, and she forgot to write to her parents. When she wrote the following letter, the homesickness she had felt only a few months earlier was apparently gone:

Medford, Sept. 30, 1797

Dear Mother:

You mentioned in yours, of the 16th inst. that it was a long time since you had received a letter from me; but it was owing to my studies which took up the greater part of my time; for I have been busy in my Arithmetic, but I finished it yesterday, and expect now to begin my large manuscript Arithmetic. You say that you shall regret so long an absence; not more certainly than I shall, but a strong desire to possess more useful knowledge than I at present do, I can dispense with the pleasure a little longer of beholding my friends and I hope I shall be better prepared to meet my good parents towards whom my heart overflows with gratitude.

Your ever affectionate daughter

ELIZA SOUTHGATE

Eliza's devotion to her work led her to ask her parents if she could continue her education at a better school. After studying for nine months at Mr. Wyman's school in Medford, Massachusetts, Eliza spent "a quarter" at Susanna Rowson's Young Ladies Academy in Boston. This school was one of the best academies of the day. It was headed by an accomplished woman of letters who was then famous as an actress, musician, playwright, and novelist. The variety and high quality of Rowson's publications marked her as one of the foremost female writers of the new United States. The appearance and popularity of their works also signaled that for the first time women had become prominent in the American literary scene.

Rowson is best known as the author of *Charlotte Temple* (London, 1791; Philadelphia, 1794), which is now known as the first American best-seller. The plot, a common one for the day, involved the seduction and betrayal of an innocent young woman by a scoundrel. Rowson, however, used this familiar material to criticize, implicitly, the sexual roles of women and men in the late 18th century. In addition to *Charlotte Temple* and a number of other novels, plays, and morality tales, Rowson wrote textbooks out of her dissatisfaction with available offerings and her devotion to teaching her students well. They included *An Abridgement of Universal Geography, together with Sketches of History* (circa 1805); *A Spelling Dictionary* (1807); and *Biblical Dialogues between a Father and His Family* (1822).

Susanna Rowson not only wrote books and ran a school for young women but also wrote and acted in plays. Rowson's last stage appearance was in her own play Americans in England, or Lessons for Daughters.

Rowson's students generally adored her, and Eliza Southgate was no exception. She wrote to her father, "I am again placed at school under the tuition of an amiable lady, so mild, so good, no one can help loving her; she treats all her scholars with such a tenderness as would win the affection of the most savage brute.... I never was happier in my life I think, and my heart overflows toward my heavenly Father for it." No doubt Eliza would have preferred to spend more time at the Boston academy, but her year of study was up in May 1798. She then returned to her family without a coveted diploma.

To receive a diploma from one of the female academies, girls had to pass examinations in the subjects covered by the curriculum. These tests were given over a number of days, and aroused a great deal of anxiety in the students, judging by the letters they wrote to their relatives. As one student, Margaret Akerly, complained to her sister, "I have so much to learn I dont know what to do with myself I hardly know what I write I think of nothing only what I have to learn; this morning I was up at 4 oClock sitting by the Lamp studying & every night I have 3 or 4 books under my head." (One wonders if Margaret passed her examination in grammar, given the poor use of punctuation in her letter.)

Graduation ceremonies often included speeches by the valedictorian and salutatorian. Such occasions marked one of the rare opportunities 18th-century girls or women had to deliver public speeches. Copies of some of the speeches have survived and show that the orators saw themselves as leaders, but leaders without a future. Although girls strove for academic excellence, they had nowhere to

T H E

RISE AND PROGRESS

O F   T H E

Young-Ladies' Academy

OF PHILADELPHIA:

Containing an Account of a Number of

PUBLIC EXAMINATIONS & COMMENCEMENTS;

The Charter and Bye-Laws;

Likewife, A Number of ORATIONS delivered

By the YOUNG LADIES,

And feveral by the *Truftees* of faid Inftitution.

———————————

P H I L A D E L P H I A :

Printed by STEWART & COCHRAN, No. 34, South Second-ftreet

M,DCC,XCIV.

In this 1794 booklet, the Young Ladies' Academy of Philadelphia printed the texts of the graduation orations and public examinations of its students as well as the history of the school.

employ their educations after graduation. Colleges were closed to women during this era, and so were the professions. Women might become skilled healers, but they could not attend medical school and become licensed physicians. They might offer religious instruction in their homes, but they could not serve as ministers for any congregations, except those of the Quakers. They might run successful businesses as single women, but when they married, the law demanded that they have their husbands' permission to continue working outside the home.

The one option open to women in the early years of the United States was marriage and motherhood. Most women accepted their role without complaint. Family life offered them many comforts. But it could not satisfy their intellectual longings, and even in the first generation of academy-educated girls and women, some pressed for change. For example, in her salutatory address to the Philadelphia Young Ladies' Academy in 1793, Priscilla Mason argued against social customs that gave men (to whom she refers as "lords") the right to control women's lives:

> Our high and mighty Lords (thanks to their arbitrary constitutions) have denied us the means of knowledge, and then reproached us for the want of it. Being the stronger party, they early seized the sceptre and the sword; with these they gave laws to society; they denied women the advantage of a liberal education; forbid them to exercise their talents on those great occasions, which would serve to improve them.... Happily, a more liberal way of thinking beings to prevail. The sources of knowledge are gradually opening to our sex.... But supposing now that we posses'd all the talents of the orator, in the highest perfection; where shall we find a theatre for the display of them? The Church, the Bar, and the Senate are shut against us. Who shut them? Man; despotic man, first made us incapable of the duty, and then forbid us the exercise. Let us by suitable education, qualify ourselves for those high departments—they will open before us.

As a Quaker, Mason went on to explain that for members of that sect, a forum for female religious oratory was already available. Unlike other churches of the era, the Society of Friends encouraged women as well as men to offer religious instruction during meeting, as they called their religious services. Women, like men, could become ministers and travel as missionaries to preach the faith. Through separate women's meetings, they were also responsible for overseeing certain areas of family life, including marriage, inheritance, and the management of children. Indeed, women with Quaker backgrounds often served as leaders in the early women's rights movement in the United States. Their work experience in the Society of Friends had prepared them to be leaders in a culture that expected women to be silent, especially in public.

But even among Quakers, women were not considered the equals of men and generally played secondary roles. Although the education of girls such as Priscilla Mason led them to expect further significant gains for women in the near future, these did not materialize. Each step forward for women took time and a great deal of effort on the part of individuals. Sometimes an apparent gain in women's rights was followed by backsliding, and retrenchment made it even harder to push forward again.

One such temporary advance occurred in New Jersey in 1776. At the height of revolutionary fervor, the state wrote its first constitution. Although other states granted the right to vote only to men, the delegates to New Jersey's constitutional convention extended the franchise to "all free inhabitants." As one state representative

Westtown Boarding School, a coeducational institution founded in 1799, was one of the most important Quaker schools in Pennsylvania. Especially designed to educate rural women, it taught "domestic employments" as well as academic subjects.

A meeting of the Society of Friends, or Quakers, in the late 18th century. The Quakers granted control over matters of inheritance and family discipline to women and, unlike most churches of the time, encouraged women to preach. As in most congregations of the era, men and women sat separately, in large part to preserve female modesty.

explained, "Our Constitution gives this right to maids or widows *black or white*." Wives were excluded because they were seen as less capable of independent action than single women. Most people assumed that a married woman would vote as her husband told her to, not as her own conscience dictated. Unmarried women, whether spinsters or widows, would not feel so compelled to follow the instructions of male relatives and friends. They would act for themselves at the polls, just as they did in managing their private affairs.

These attitudes reflected theories about women's property rights. The eminent English legal authority Sir William Blackstone had explained the legal position of married women this way in his *Commentaries on the Laws of England*, which was published shortly before the Revolution: "By marriage, the husband and wife are one person in law; that is, the very being or legal existence of the woman is suspended during the marriage, or at least is incorporated and consolidated into that of the husband; under whose wing, protection, and *cover* she performs every thing."

Under the laws of England as enforced in the United States, married women could not own property in their own name without special (and rare) contracts called marriage settlements. Everything a woman brought to marriage became her husband's. Movable goods became her husband's absolutely, and a man could sell or give away his wife's movables at will. Men's control over women's real estate was restricted, however. A husband could not mortgage or sell his wife's land unless the woman consented and signed deeds stating she did so of her own free will. But during marriage, a man could manage his wife's real estate and take all the rents and profits for his own use. These laws stemmed from a belief that families could be provided for best if the head of the family—the man—controlled all of the family's assets. In exchange for his wife's property, a husband became legally responsible for providing his wife with the necessities of life. If he neglected her, a woman could sue for support and be protected by the courts.

Restrictions on the political rights of married women flowed naturally from restrictions on their property rights. Just as men were obliged under the law to support their wives financially, the political system of the age assumed that husbands represented their wives as well as themselves when they cast their votes. The couple acted as a unit, represented by the husband. A second argument against allowing married women to vote was that they were not viewed as independent persons. Political theorists regarded women as incapable of exercising the franchise because they were subject to their husbands' influence. As one commentator asked, "How can a fair one refuse her lover?"

For the same reason, men without property also could not vote. Just like women, they were not independent persons. To earn a living, they were forced to work for others, and therefore their votes might be coerced or purchased.

Given these commonly held assumptions about women's rights, the New Jersey Constitution of 1776 was a surprise. In this state alone, revolutionary leaders extended the democratic ideal to include women. The restriction of their reform to single women "worth fifty pounds clear estate" and over the age of 21 is consistent with the theories of the day. The fact that they gave the vote to any women at all is not. What happened?

According to some historians, the New Jersey delegates were influenced by revolutionary ideals of justice more than anything else. They firmly believed that property holders of either sex should have a vote. By giving some women, but not all men, the vote, they were

This noncontemporary print shows women voting in New Jersey after the Revolution. Women lost the vote when male politicians began to fear their political influence.

upholding the sanctity of property. They also were acknowledging the growth of women's political awareness during the war and the tremendous sacrifices made by New Jersey women in the early campaigns. Finally, Quakers, who believed in the equality of the sexes, had a strong influence in state politics during this period. The franchise clause probably was drafted by John Cooper, a prominent Quaker.

This explanation has not proved convincing to all historians of revolutionary era women. Some believe the initial wording of the New Jersey Constitution was an oversight rather than a deliberate step to enfranchise women. They argue that belief in the political subservience of women was too firmly entrenched to allow such a radical step to occur, particularly without public commentary in the press. Instead, they argue, women took advantage of the loose wording of the constitution. Voting regularly in local and statewide elections over the years, they gradually established a legal precedent that male politicians could not ignore. By 1790, when the state wrote a new election law, the men were ready to define voters explicitly as "he or she." As the statesman Elias Boudinot proclaimed in a Fourth of July oration delivered in Elizabeth Town, New Jersey, in 1793, "The rights of women are no longer strange sounds to an American ear, and I devoutly hope the day is not far distant when we shall find them dignifying in a distinguishing code, the jurisprudence of several states of the Union."

During the years when women were enfranchised in New Jersey, they seized the opportunity to act independently. Women's names appeared on town voting lists, newspaper reports noted the appearance of women at the polls, and political detractors and supporters of female suffrage alike commented on women's political activities. Women in other states expressed their envy of New Jersey women. One, Susan Boudinot Bradford, wrote, "I congratulate the ladies of New Jersey that they are in some thing put on a footing with the gentlemen and the most extraordinary part [of] it is, that it has been done by the gentlemen themselves but these are a few who have been more enlightened than the rest."

In fact, the very success of female suffrage in New Jersey contributed to its demise. After the establishment of America's first political parties (the Federalists and the Republicans) in 1789, women became an interest group courted by politicians, especially in close elections. Each party feared that the other would gain the support of women. And each side derided women's participation in elections when they thought they had been hurt by it but at the next election attempted once again to gain the support of women.

In the election of 1800, for example, Federalists Alexander Hamilton and Senator Matthias Ogden "so ingratiated themselves in the esteem of the Federalist ladies of Elizabeth-town, and in the lower part of the state," a Newark newspaper reported, "as to induce them (as it is said) to resolve on turning out to support the Federal ticket in the ensuing elections." Meanwhile, Republican politicians tried to win women voters with fiery speeches. As one orator proclaimed, "Our daughters are the same relation to us as our sons; we owe them the same duties; they have the same science, and are equally competent to their attainments. The contrary idea originated in the same abuse of power, as monarchy and slavery, and owes its little remaining support to stale sophistry." He then recited a long list of heroic women who had proved the equality of

The "Ladies Patriotic Song" (1798) was set to the tune of "Washington's March at the Battle of Trenton." In a highly traditional vein, the songwriter saw it as women's role to use love, beauty, and innocence to inspire men to patriotic deeds.

the sexes by their actions and writings. The speaker concluded, "The history of women is forever obtruding on our unwilling eyes bold and ardent spirits, who no tyrant could tame—no prejudice enslave.... Female-Citizens, follow examples so glorious; accept the station nature intended for you, and double the knowledge and happiness of mankind." They could do that best, he claimed, by voting for the Republican ticket.

Women continued to participate in New Jersey politics until 1807, when the election law was rewritten. Women, blacks, and aliens lost the vote at that time. The wording of the election law was part of a compromise between liberal and conservative Republicans, who had gained political control of the state but were in danger of losing power over their party. The move also was part of a widespread cultural shift away from radicalism. New Jerseyans, like Americans generally, did not want to face the full social implications of their revolutionary heritage. No other state had imitated New Jersey's example by giving women the vote. Elsewhere, even as slavery was abolished in the North, blacks were losing the franchise and other basic rights. Americans had their republic. But they were not yet ready to make it a full democracy.

During this era, all other legal reforms affecting white women focused exclusively on their private lives. (For black women, the end of slavery in the North was the most significant postrevolutionary reform.) One of the most important of these legal changes concerned divorce. Under English law as enforced in the colonies, absolute divorces that gave couples the right to remarry were virtually impossible to obtain. They were available only to men and required two procedures. First, a man had to sue his wife for adultery and obtain a conviction in an ecclesiastical, or church, court. Then, he had to obtain a private act of Parliament giving him the right to remarry. These suits and petitions were so expensive that only wealthy Englishmen could seek them. The poor, who cared less about their reputations and had little property to worry about, practiced informal divorce. One spouse, usually the husband, simply deserted, and both spouses entered into new, technically illegal unions. Friends and relatives condoned such behavior, and informal marriages were common in both England and America. But women and men between the highest and the lowest ranks of society had no solution to the problem of an unhappy marriage.

After the Revolution, all the new states made divorces easier to obtain. Some legislatures voted to allow both formal separations with property divisions, and absolute divorces that permitted remarriage. Others provided only for separations. But everywhere it was acknowledged that women and men needed legal recourse for disastrous marriages. As Pennsylvania lawmakers wrote in the preamble to that state's 1785 divorce statute, "It is the design of marriage, and the wish of parties entering into that state that it should continue during their joint lives, yet where one party is... guilty of acts and deeds inconsistent with the nature thereof, the laws of every well regulated society ought to give relief to the innocent and injured person." Freedom from English law allowed Americans to institute reforms in marriage that England adopted only in the 20th century.

Both women and men benefited from the new laws, which acknowledged male as well as female adultery and prohibited physical cruelty. American lawmakers congratulated themselves on their liberality to the female sex, but the courts still favored men. They routinely demanded more evidence of men's wrongdoing than women's and automatically gave men custody of their children.

Revolutionary ideals led to few other improvements in the status of women immediately following the war. For the most part,

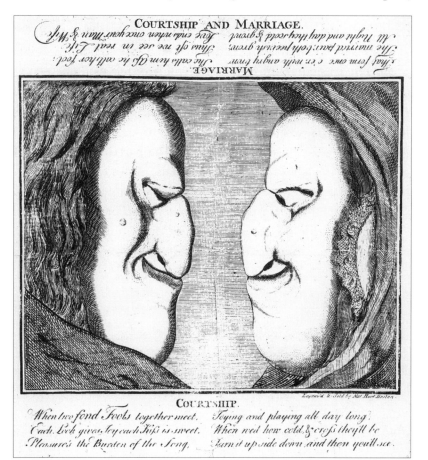

A satirical print uses a visual pun to contrast Courtship and Marriage. Right side up, the smiling faces bear the caption "When two fond fools together meet, Each Look gives Joy each Kiss is sweet." Turned upside down, the same faces scowl, with the caption "The married pair both peevish grow, All Night and day they scold & growl."

Americans seemed intent on recreating the kind of stable sexual relationships they had known before the war, relationships in which women were subservient to men. Female independence and initiative, valued during a time of war, were less desirable when the crisis had passed. Perhaps Americans feared changing too much in their lives all at once. By being conservative on sexual issues, they may have felt freer to pursue radical political reforms.

Sexual equality has proved to be a very difficult goal to achieve in the United States. Not until the 19th century were property laws gradually changed to give women independent rights to real and personal property. Women were granted voting privileges even later, in 1920. And even today the laws on marriage, divorce, and the family have not resolved all issues of inequality.

Nevertheless, probably the most important first step on the road to sexual equality was taken after the Revolution. Higher education for women gave them the means to work for their own independence. As soon as women could demonstrate that their intellectual abilities were equal to men's, denying them legal and political rights became increasingly difficult. The founding of female academies at the end of the 18th century, then, marked the beginning of a new era for women. As Judith Sargent Murray, an early advocate of women's higher education, wrote in 1798: "I expect to see our young women forming a new era in female history.... The partial distribution of advantages which has too long obtained, is, in this enlightened age, rapidly giving place to a more uniform system of information ... and *the revolution of events is advancing in that half of the human species, which hath hitherto been involved in the night of darkness, toward the irradiating sun of science.*"

As an essayist and advocate of sexual equality, Judith Sargent Murray (1751–1820) contributed to the early national debate on the value of higher education for women. She argued forcefully that because women were raised from birth to be dependent on men, they and their families were placed in unnecessary danger. Poorly educated, with little or no vocational training, most women were unprepared to give either their parents or their husband meaningful help in providing for their family. If they became widows, which was common in the 18th century, women needed to settle their husband's estate and care for their children on their own. Yet most women possessed only a rudimentary education and were taught to think of themselves as helpless outside of the domestic sphere. To avoid the dangers of female dependence, Murray argued that girls should be given better educations. Not only would schooling improve their minds but it also would give them the skills necessary to help support themselves and their families. Murray adamantly opposed frivolous, decorative education for girls. She maintained that female students needed to study accounting rather than music, and that history was more important for training the mind than French. Murray's assumption that most women would marry and therefore find their primary vocation in domestic labor demonstrates the limits of feminist thought after the Revolution. Even advocates of women's equality could not envision true female independence at this time.

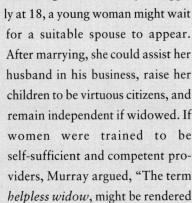

Judith Sargent Murray

Murray believed that many young women rushed into marriage before reaching maturity as a way of avoiding the humiliation of spinsterhood. She believed that if they could achieve financial independence and support themselves prior to marriage, they would be free to choose their mates more intelligently. Rather than feeling forced to marry unhappily at 18, a young woman might wait for a suitable spouse to appear. After marrying, she could assist her husband in his business, raise her children to be virtuous citizens, and remain independent if widowed. If women were trained to be self-sufficient and competent providers, Murray argued, "The term *helpless widow*, might be rendered as unfrequent and inapplicable as that of *helpless widower;* and although we should undoubtedly continue to mourn . . . yet we should derive consolation from the knowledge . . . that a mother could *assist* as well as *weep* over her offspring."

Murray's essays on female equality, education, religion, politics, and the social customs of her age appeared originally in periodicals such as the *Gentleman's and Lady's Town and Country Magazine* and *Massachusetts Magazine.* In 1798 these essays were gathered together into a three-volume set called *The Gleaner* and sold by subscription. George Washington's name headed the list of those who contracted to buy the books before publication. Judith Sargent Murray became one of the foremost social commentators of her age by demonstrating clearly to her contemporaries that women were the intellectual equals of men.

CHAPTER 5

THE LIMITS OF REPUBLICANISM: RACIAL CONFLICTS IN THE NORTH, SOUTH, AND WEST

Republican ideas of freedom and equality led to the gradual abolition of slavery in the North, but not in the South and the opening West. African Americans across the nation were quick to argue that slavery had no place in a republic. But only in areas where whites owned few slaves and where the economy was not dependent on slave labor did courts and legislatures act to outlaw human bondage. The Constitution supported slavery, in acknowledgment of the financial dependence of many areas on a slave work force. As practiced in the new United States, then, democracy was limited by the economic interests of slaveholding whites.

In the years following the Revolution, slavery as an institution grew and strengthened in the South. The rationale for slavery changed and hardened, becoming explicitly racist in tone. The potential for revolutionary change present in the republican ideals of the era was not, therefore, realized.

Northern states acted separately to end slavery. Vermont was the first state to forbid it by incorporating an antislavery provision into its 1777 constitution. In Massachusetts the courts abolished slavery in a series of "freedom cases" brought by slaves and their sympathizers in the 1780s. As Chief Justice William Cushing of the

Frequently, white children captured by Native American tribes resisted being returned to their own families. In this engraving by the prominent artist Benjamin West, a young boy shows his dismay at being forced to leave his adopted Indian mother.

Samuel Jennings painted Liberty Displaying the Arts and Sciences *in 1792 for the Free Library of Philadelphia. The Library requested an abolitionist theme and suggested this representation of the Goddess of Liberty offering symbols of the arts to a group of free black Americans.*

Supreme Judicial Court ruled, "The idea of slavery is inconsistent with our own conduct and constitution .... there can be no such thing as perpetual servitude of a rational creature." New Hampshire adopted a constitution in 1783 that declared "all men are born equal and independent." Although no court cases tested the meaning of these words, slavery in New Hampshire disappeared over the next two decades. Only eight slaves were listed in the New Hampshire census of 1800; in the 1810 census there were none.

Elsewhere the process of freeing the enslaved was painfully slow. State legislatures enacted gradual abolition statutes in Pennsylvania (1780), Rhode Island (1784), Connecticut (1784), New York (1799), and New Jersey (1804). These laws provided for the freedom of the children of slaves when they reached ages ranging from 18 to 28. In this way, parents who were enslaved for life saw their children become free. Their victory must have been bittersweet, filled with both joy and agonizing frustration. As late as 1840, New Jersey still listed legally owned slaves on its census.

In response to political pressure and their own personal dislike of slavery, some southern slaveholders and northern owners of adult slaves freed their slaves. Antislavery legislation, combined with these private actions, produced a large free black population in the United States by the beginning of the 19th century. Many more free blacks lived in the Chesapeake area than in the Carolinas or Georgia, but everywhere their numbers grew. As a consequence, black slaves could escape to freedom more easily than ever before. They could now pose as free during their flights and also use the homes of free friends and relatives as hiding places. Before the war, escape had been virtually impossible. Now the North Star became a guide to a free land.

For women, the shift from slave to free status had momentous importance, even more so than for men. Beyond giving women the right to choose where and for whom they would work, freedom gave them control over their persons and their children for the first time. Black women could now defend themselves more effectively from sexual assault. They could live with their own family separately from whites, thereby denying white men easy access. And if they were raped by a white or black assailant, they could bring a suit in a court of law, an option that was not available to them under slavery. Abolition did not end the sexual abuse of black women, but it did limit it in important ways. Just as significant, free women could face childbirth with a different set of expectations. No longer did they have to fear forced separation from their children.

Freedom did not, however, change the daunting work responsibilities of black women. They remained largely an unskilled work force. Under the southern slave system, women worked almost exclusively as agricultural laborers. A few found employment as domestics, and on rare occasions (especially during the war years) women worked at skilled tasks, such as spinning and weaving. But many more black men than women worked at skilled trades under slavery. In the North the story had been much the same. Most women who lived in urban areas worked as unskilled domestics, but if they lived in rural areas they worked in the fields.

Benjamin Latrobe, a British architect who worked on the U.S. Capitol, made this watercolor sketch of "An Overseer Doing His Duty" in Fredericksburg, Virginia. Most slave women worked at hard labor in the fields of the South.

After the Revolution, many rural black women migrated to northern towns and cities. Like white women faced with the necessity of supporting themselves, they learned they could find work there more easily. As a result, African-American women outnumbered men in northern urban areas at the end of the 18th century.

For a few of these women the move brought opportunity. For the first time some African-American women began to support themselves as retailers, boardinghouse keepers, bakers, peddlers, and teachers. But only 1 in 20 found these types of jobs. Most former slaves found that freedom gave them little opportunity to raise their standard of living. Most black women in towns and cities worked as laundresses. As the Pennsylvania Abolition Society reported in 1795, "The Women generally, both married and single, wash clothes for a living." This physically demanding job was no easier than fieldwork. Whatever their occupation, under both slavery and freedom women worked from dawn to dusk to support themselves and their families. Among blacks, as among poor whites, the contribution of all

Above: Free black women held menial jobs, often as scrubwomen. This one was depicted by Baroness Hyde de Neville, the wife of a French diplomat.

Left: Free blacks were highly entrepreneurial. Street vendors in Philadelphia sold pepper-pot soup, a local specialty, to supplement the family income.

family members was needed to survive.

Life in northern towns and cities did have one significant advantage: the existence of close-knit black communities, which provided emotional and financial support to people in need. In all urban centers blacks moved gradually into their own neighborhoods. At first they sought simple companionship, the opportunity to live with people who did not judge them as inferiors. Soon, however, they were establishing churches, schools, and charitable societies to help each other in their daily struggles for survival. Life in the urban North was difficult for black families, but for those who could live where they wanted and with whom they wanted for the first time, freedom made the daily struggle to survive worthwhile.

Unfortunately, many newly freed blacks did not have the resources to move into their own homes. Most enslaved black women had worked as domestic servants and lived in the homes of their owners. With no savings and low wages, some were obliged to re-

Elizabeth Freeman, a slave in Massachusetts, sued for her freedom. After succeeding in court, she went to work for wages in the home of her lawyer and eventually purchased her own home.

main where they were after emancipation. Many whites made residence in their homes a condition of employment. Some controlled the behavior of their servants outside the house as well. In the first generation after slavery, therefore, some women still experienced little personal freedom.

For others, however, living separately from whites was their greatest priority. As soon as they learned they were free, they walked away without looking back. They had been waiting so long for freedom and had suffered so much as slaves that they had to strike out on their own, surviving off the land or charity until they found employment and places to live.

Reports of freedom cases such as that of the Massachusetts slave Elizabeth Freeman, also known as Mumbet, had electrifying effects on some blacks. The following story tells of how one typical woman might have been inspired to start a new life:

Once I heard about Mumbet I just walked off the place. Master couldn't keep me there because us slaves were free. Mumbet won herself the right in the courts. That judge said she was a free woman who could work where she wanted. And she made me a free woman too. I knew that. Didn't take much figuring. Massachusetts allowed no white people to own us after that Revolution. We were all free. So we started to move, and we mostly, us women, moved to the towns if we could. Took our youngins and went. Except some had to stay where they were, because they had no friends or family in Boston or Salem or places like that. Some people been staying with white folks for a long time, and it's frustrating. But they have masters that cause them no trouble, and it's better to stay where they are. Particularly women who have husbands and youngins with them.

But me, I went because I had enough of master. He was so bad there wasn't no living with him. Got myself a job right off. Washing, that's all. Lived with my sister and her friends and there were about ten or twelve of us in that little house. But we were free, that's all. We were glad. Then I met my husband. His name is Benjamin Smith. Before the Revolution they called him Ben. All the time Ben, and boy. He didn't like that. So now he's Benjamin, a full and proper name. And me, I changed my name too. Was Queenie. Now I'm

Elizabeth. Elizabeth Smith. I say it real careful 'cause it's important, your name. Mumbet, she changed her name to Elizabeth, so I did too, 'cause I love that woman so much. Benjamin works on the ships that go from Boston to Philadelphia. He's a good sailor, and works hard and I've got no complaints. Except he's gone from home most of the time. I still work all the time, sometimes washing, sometimes cleaning, sometimes picking rags. My babies go with me and my older girl she helps. We're getting by, and we've got a better place to live, just with my sister and her family. Except we're always taking in new folks, from the country, who have no place else to go. Especially women. Set them up. Get them started. I watch out for the women.

Another thing I want to say. We have a church now. The African Zion Church, we call it. We all put our cents in and after awhile we got enough to buy a little land. Had to. Whites don't want us in their churches, and especially don't want us burying our dead in their churchyards. And we need a place for our dead. It's not right, putting them in the poor folks burying ground as though they don't belong to no one. It's not right, 'cause your ancestors are important. They have to be buried right. And you have to take care of their graves, and watch over their bones. Or you'll be in trouble when your time comes. So, myself and my sister and Benjamin and the other people in this part of town, we started to build a church. And it is just small. Just a shack really. But we've got a preacher even the whites like. They ask him to preach at their meetings sometimes, and he does. And I know why. He says it's good for the whites to know black folks have the ways of the Lord in their hearts. And he is a great preacher. And we all appreciate his work. And he travels sometimes and we miss him, but then he comes back here. There are not enough black preachers for all the folks who want to know the ways of the Lord. Yes, we're doing better, really. Except the white folks still have lots of hate in them. Us free people have to be careful all the time. It's no good, still, between us blacks and the whites.

The rise of a large free black population in the North aggravated racial tensions in both the North and South. White northerners no longer wanted to uphold a slave system, but for the most part their attitudes toward the newly freed slaves did not change. Racist feelings of superiority determined the treatment of blacks under both slavery and freedom. And as slavery became even more firmly entrenched in the South, explicitly racist arguments in favor of the institution were heard more and more. White southerners argued that blacks were intellectually incapable of caring for themselves and their families. They claimed that blacks were inherently lazy, dishonest, and foolish. If blacks were on their own, these whites maintained, they would stop working and turn to lives of petty crime. According to these arguments, whites were fulfilling a vital social obligation by keeping blacks enslaved.

Although northern whites saw daily evidence that free blacks were capable and hardworking, they readily accepted southern judgments on the inferiority of African Americans. Such beliefs allowed

Space was at a premium in the holds of slave ships, which sometimes lost a third of their cargo to death en route. The ships were not as clean as this image indicates, but were rife with sewage and disease.

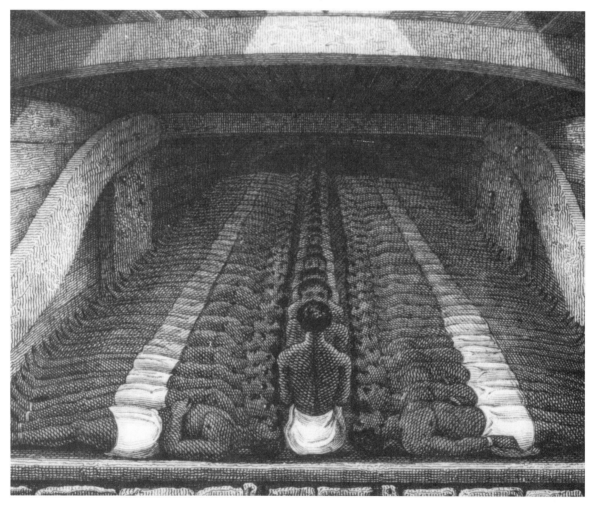

them to deny blacks basic rights, including the rights to vote, own real estate, and go to school. Racism solved a moral dilemma for some whites. If they believed in the inferiority of African Americans, they were relieved of the obligation to help them build better lives for themselves as free people.

After the Revolution the black population grew rapidly in the American South. Devastated by years of warfare, small farmers and large planters alike began rebuilding their work forces. Those with the means immediately purchased slaves to replace the ones they had lost during the war. Poorer farmers had to wait. As the economy improved, the demand for workers increased suddenly while the supply remained the same. As they had in the colonial period, southerners turned to the slave trade to solve their labor shortage. Tragically, as slavery ended in the North, it expanded in the South through the forced enslavement of thousands of newly imported Africans.

The U.S. Constitution allowed this importation. Although some political leaders had advocated the closing of the slave trade, a compromise was reached. Slaves could be brought into the United States during the 20 years following the Constitution's ratification. As stated in Article I, Section 9, "The migration or importation of such persons as any of the States now existing shall think proper to admit shall not be prohibited by the Congress prior to the year 1808." Tens of thousands of new slaves came to the United States in those two decades.

With the end of legal slave importation in sight, the role of enslaved women as childbearers took on new importance. By the end of the 18th century slave owners understood that their slaves' fertility increased their wealth and guaranteed the continued prosperity of their children. As Thomas Jefferson remarked, "I consider a woman who brings a child every two years as more profitable than the best man of the farm." This attitude became particularly prevalent in Maryland, Delaware, and Virginia, where planters began to encourage slaves to have large families as a way of making money.

Slave owners such as Jefferson offered women rewards for marrying and for frequently bearing children. On one occasion he directed his overseer to give a newly married slave woman a cooking pot and a bed—presents meant to indicate his approval of her choice of one of his other enslaved workers as a husband. Jefferson also

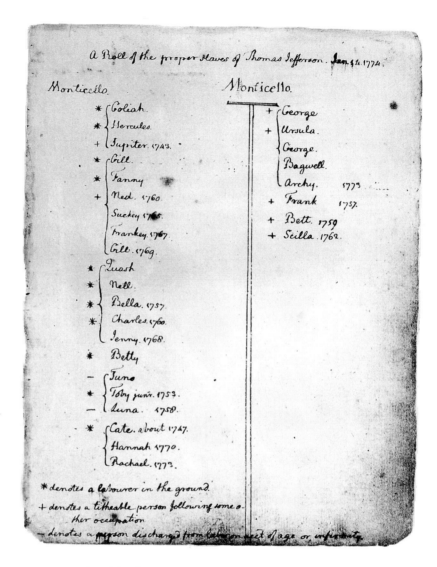

Thomas Jefferson listed the slaves at his Monticello, Virginia, plantation, by first names only. He noted which were grounds workers (those with asterisks), which engaged in other occupations (with plus signs), and which were retired (with minus signs).

encouraged stable slave marriages. He once wrote, "There is nothing I desire so much as that all the young people in the estate should intermarry with one another and stay at home." People who married "at home" were "worth a great deal more ... than when they have husbands and wives abroad." Jefferson realized that marriages between his own workers allowed them to live more contentedly under the yoke of slavery.

Other men went even further to encourage slave women to marry and to bear children. One Virginia planter promised his slave Jenny that he would give her freedom if she bore six children—the number of offspring he had. He kept his word. After Jenny delivered her

sixth child in eleven years, she and her youngest child gained their freedom in 1803. Imagine this woman's position. She was free, but her other five children remained enslaved for life.

In other cases, white men coerced their female slaves into reproducing. Some women found themselves coupled with a man unwillingly, simply because the master said it was time for them to produce children. Many owners even raped their own slaves or forced them to become their mistresses. Tragically, most of these men later turned the offspring from these unions into slaves. The social system of the southern colonies and states frowned on men who acknowledged their sexual liaisons by granting freedom to their children.

Even the slave owners who promoted stable family life took little trouble to ensure that families stayed together. Although planters might try to keep slave families intact while their children were young, older children generally were the first to be sold off the home plantation. One Charleston man explained his decision to sell a female slave this way: "She has a practice of goeing frequently to her Father and Mother, who Live at a Plantation I am concern'd in, about Twenty Miles from Town." Rather than respecting this young woman's

Although slave marriages were technically not legal, some African-American couples celebrated in their own tradition, jumping over a broomstick to seal their union.

In one of several scenes illustrating an antislavery publication, the artist depicts one of the worst abominations of slavery: a slaveholder taking slave children away from their mother, presumably for sale.

clear desire to be with her family, the owner put her on a ship for Lisbon, Portugal, where she was sold.

On large plantations, where slaves lived and worked on different land holdings, adolescents often lived apart from their parents and grandparents. Frequently lonely, these children missed their older relatives' help in dealing with the cruelties of slavery. Nevertheless, slave parents and grandparents did whatever they could to protect the younger generation. For instance, when one elderly woman learned that her granddaughter had been beaten by an overseer, she asked her master to move the girl to another section of the plantation managed by a different overseer. After the master refused, the woman punished him in her own way. As the master reported the incident, "Sukey, the old Granny ... to be revenged because I would not take her granddaughter away turned out all my Cattle last night on my Cowpen ground which have done me a prodigeous mischief. She has had the impudence to say the child is poor and starved when I declare I never saw a finer, well, fat, nor healthyer child. I will repay this treatment." Undoubtedly, this slave woman received a whipping for attempting to help her granddaughter. Had she lived nearby, she could have assisted the child in more useful ways than by pleading with an unsympathetic owner.

One of the most tragic aspects of the slave system was the help-lessness of women such as Sukey to prevent the breakup of their families. Encouraged to produce children, most slave women experienced the agony of forced separation from their daughters and sons. Sojourner Truth, an abolitionist who was born at the end of the 18th century, explained her own despair to audiences at antislavery meetings in the years leading up to the outbreak of the Civil War in 1861. In her most famous speech, which was recorded by a white listener, she cried,

Abolitionist Sojourner Truth also worked for equal rights for women. She said, "Supose a man's mind holds a quart, and a woman's don't hold but a pint; if her pint is full, it's as good as his quart."

> Dat man ober dar say dat womin needs to be helped into carriages, and lifted ober ditches, and to hab de best place everywhar. Nobody eber helps me into carriages, or ober mud-puddles, or gibs me any best place! And a'n't I a woman? Look at me! Look at my arm! I have ploughed, and planted, and gathered into barns, and no man could head me! And a'n't I a woman? I could work as much and eat as much as a man—when I could get it—and bear de lash as well! And a'n't I a woman? I have borne thirteen chilern, and seen 'em mos' all sold off to slavery, and when I cried out with my mother's grief, none but Jesus heard me! And a'n't' I a woman?

Although enslaved women usually could not prevent owners from making decisions about their workers based on economic considerations, they never gave up trying. As mothers, daughters, sisters, and wives, women protested, complained, and pushed the boundaries of acceptable behavior whenever they could. For example, even though Virginia planter Robert Carter believed in "moderate correction in every case," he was forced to reconsider his ideas after an overzealous driver mistreated a slave child. After the child's mother complained to Carter, he admitted that "in the present case...allowances for the feelings of a Mother" should have been made. By forcing owners to acknowledge maternal love, women sustained themselves and their families emotionally. They could not prevent the suffering of their children and grandchildren, but they could protest it. In the process they maintained the affection and the will of family members.

In giving birth to children under slavery, women affirmed their life-giving force. No white person could destroy their power and determination to produce life, to survive despite the hardships of slavery in the American South. Although some women practiced abortion and infanticide to deny owners additional human property, many more bore children as a means of self-affirmation. In African-American culture, as in the traditional societies of West Africa from which these people came, motherhood gave women personal fulfillment and high social status. As wives and mothers, they satisfied their own needs and the needs of black slave communities even more than the needs of owners. Enslaved families, however tortured, produced the means for individual slave survival.

Just as African-American women struggled to defend their families under slavery, Native American women attempted to protect their families from total destruction during the revolutionary era. The war was very hard on the eastern tribes, which suffered attacks from both English and Patriot troops. Some Indians tried to stay neutral, but the stance proved impossible to maintain. And no matter which side a tribe joined in the war, the enemy loomed near.

The Iroquois's experiences reflect those of all the eastern tribes at the end of the 18th century. During the Revolution, the Iroquois Confederacy could not agree on whom to support in the war. Initially, the Iroquois were neutral because it was unclear whether participating in the war on either side could work to their benefit. But by the summer of 1777 many of the Indians had rethought their position. The Oneida and Tuscarora chose to remain neutral, which at that point meant they were effectively siding with the Americans. But warriors from the Seneca, Cayuga, Onondaga, and Mohawk tribes decided to join the British, and "the mothers also consented to it," as the Seneca warrior Blacksnake reported. The final decision to go to war was made not by the chiefs, but by the warriors and the respected older women whose sacrifice of sons, brothers, and husbands was acknowledged in Iroquois political culture.

Immediately after joining the British, Iroquois warriors participated in a major battle at Oriskany, New York, in which casualties were high on all sides. Neither the English nor the Americans could claim complete victory. The British had not been able to take Fort Stanwix as planned, but they did succeed in inflicting high casual-

War and Pestilence!

HORRIBLE AND UNPARALELLED
MASSACRE !

Women and Children
FALLING VICTIMS TO THE
INDIAN'S TOMAHAWK.

Using stereotyped images, a broadside printed about 1800 demonstrates white settlers' fear of Indian attack.

ties on the Patriot troops. The Indians, however, were distraught over the bloodshed and destruction without victory. They returned to their villages disillusioned with organized British warfare. Their despair was reported by Mary Jemison, a white woman who became a member of the Seneca and lived with the tribe for her entire adult life. She wrote, "Our town exhibited a scene of real sorrow and distress, when our warriors returned and recounted their misfortunes, and stated the real loss they had received in the engagement. The mourning was excessive, and was expressed by the most doleful yells, shrieks, and howlings."

For the rest of the war the Iroquois preferred to engage in traditional Indian tactics of guerrilla warfare. They attacked individual farms and small frontier settlements in swift-moving raiding parties, destroying homes and fields but killing only those male settlers who resisted them. The warriors were highly successful. By the end of the Revolution, Indian and Loyalist raiders had destroyed white settlements in an area covering nearly 50,000 square miles and stretching from the Mohawk Valley in New York to the Monongahela River in Ohio. When the English surrendered, the Iroquois were surprised and severely disappointed. From their perspective the war was going well.

Although the Iroquois warriors waged war successfully between 1778 and 1782, ultimately their campaign of destruction could not protect their people. Infuriated by their own inability to protect frontier whites, Patriot troops assumed the same tactics as the Native Americans.

A Mohawk village on the Grand River shortly after the Revolution.

Soldiers could not attack warrior bands easily, but they could destroy Iroquois towns and villages. Beginning in the summer of 1779, they systematically burned houses, outbuildings, and planted fields; cut down orchards; and dispersed the inhabitants. George Washington became known among the Iroquois as Town Destroyer for his role in directing these campaigns. By the next spring only 2 out of 30 Iroquois villages remained unharmed.

The winter of 1779–80 was one of great hardship for the Iroquois. Most of them had no homes and suffered from exposure during the bitterly cold winter. Food was scarce, and epidemics of smallpox, dysentery, and measles ravaged the camps. Iroquois warriors continued to raid white settlements throughout the following three summers. But in the meantime, those left behind—the women, the children, the sick, and the elderly—faced the steady destruction of their way of life.

The war threatened the Iroquois with extinction. Between the revolutionary era and the end of the century, the population of the Six Nations was cut approximately in half, from between eight to ten thousand to about four thousand people. Most of the dead were

In this 1807 depiction of members of the Oneida tribe, the man is presented as a hunter while the woman cares for children.

not warriors killed in battle, but people of all ages and both sexes who suffered from disease, starvation, and exposure.

Although the Iroquois survived, their culture, in many ways, did not. Peace found the Iroquois crowded on relatively small reservations, unable to follow the customs of the hunt, migration of town sites, warfare, and family relationships. As a people, they now questioned the validity of their traditions because they had fared so badly

Indian women struggled to preserve their families despite the encroachment of white civilization. In this sketch, the Indian woman's discomfort in a European-style chair symbolizes the difficulties faced by Native Americans confronting the ways of white people.

in their contests with Europeans. Many Iroquois came to despise their own culture as an inferior one without a place in a new world order.

Reservation life changed many aspects of Indian behavior. One important shift occurred in the division of labor between women and men. On reservations, men's traditional labor—hunting and warfare—lost significance. Men continued to hunt, but game was scarce and became more so as the years passed. The men usually were able to provide their families with meat, but they no longer traded in furs. In addition, accepting peace on white men's terms meant that warriors were acknowledging their inability to defend their families. As a result, political and religious leaders, as well as the warriors themselves, suffered greatly from shame. During the postrevolutionary period, alcoholism was common, stemming from depression and an absence of hope. As a missionary at the Buffalo Creek reservation in upstate New York explained, "Indians, as has been observed, bear suffering with great fortitude, but at the end of this fortitude is desperation. Suicides are frequent among the Senecas. I apprehend this despondency is the principal cause of their intemperance." Among Indian men, unrestricted drinking led to thefts, fights, and wife and child abuse. Such behavior could occur at important council meetings as well as in everyday situations. During negotiations for a major treaty with the federal government in 1797, for example, a white participant reported, "Red Jacket and many of the Indians . . . from intoxication fell to fighting in groups, pulling Hair biting like dogs w[h]ere ever they could get hold."

At about this same time a federal agent reported that "the Indians of the Six Nations ... have become given to indolence, drunkeness and thefts, and have taken to killing each other, there have been five murders among themselves within Six months—they have recd their payments and immediately expended it for liquor and in the course of a frollick have killed one or two."

Meanwhile, women also suffered from depression, and alcoholism among them was common. They had seen their homes destroyed, their fields burned, and their children die after great suffering. The drunk, "aged women, in particular . . . were often seen lying beside the paths, overcome." Like the men, they questioned themselves and the value of their traditions. But unlike the men, women still had

The Mohawk boys and girls at the Grand River school dress in European style, but the boys wear scalp locks, the traditional Mohawk hairstyle. The illustration appeared in a 1786 primer designed for Mohawk children.

some traditional patterns to fall back on. Their work roles were unchanged. They still tended their children, farmed, cooked, produced craft goods, and participated in the political decisions of their tribes. For women life on reservations meant fewer changes than it did for men. Throughout the difficult period of adjustment, they worked in their fields and found a purpose in the labor that kept their families from starvation. Thus when Quaker missionaries arrived at one reservation in the spring of 1798, they saw the women busy at their planting "while the men were standing in companies sporting themselves with their bows and arrows and other trifling amusements."

Programs initiated by the federal government and individual religious groups such as the Society of Friends encouraged Iroquois men to become farmers. The adjustment was very difficult. Most of the older men never embraced the new occupation, but young men slowly began to learn the farming techniques of the whites. A Quaker assistance program persuaded some Seneca to abandon their old ways. Missionaries from the Society of Friends built a model farm where the whites pursued their agricultural work in full view of the Indians. The Quakers were careful to point out that long ago their own ancestors had been forced to adjust to new ways but that eventually farming had made life easier for both men and women. According to the Quaker missionaries, Seneca women encouraged their men to learn to farm as whites did. At one meeting the Quakers noticed that although many of the Seneca men regarded their suggestions as comical, some others and "particularly the women" appeared "solid" in their support of the Quakers' ideas.

At the end of the 18th century a Seneca religious prophet named Handsome Lake became very influential in helping his people accept a new way of life. Respected as a messenger from the spirit world, Handsome Lake called for the reformation of Iroquois behavior. He condemned alcoholism and the practice of witchcraft. He also argued that unless the Iroquois changed, they would cease to exist as a people. His apocalyptic view was accompanied by specific instructions on what the Iroquois should do to survive. He said that men must learn to farm, and women must become good housewives who could spin and weave. Handsome Lake was able to convince many Seneca that only by following new ways could their people survive.

Many aspects of traditional male and female behavior troubled Handsome Lake. He objected to men's physical abuse of their wives and children (especially when the men were drunk), the adultery of both spouses, and the prevalence of divorce. He urged his people to change their attitudes toward the nuclear family—a household con-

Handsome Lake Preaching

Handsome Lake, holding a wampum belt, preaches to a meeting of the Longhouse religion. He helped the Indians of New York State adapt to white customs such as male dominance of the nuclear family.

sisting only of a mother, a father, and their children. Under traditional Iroquois teachings the kin relationship between mother and daughter took precedence over all others. Handsome Lake now maintained that the husband-wife bond must take first place in people's loyalties. He believed that most problems between wives and husbands stemmed from the interference of mothers, and he taught that "The Creator is sad because of the tendency of old women to breed mischief." According to the prophet, mothers encouraged daughters to argue with their husbands; they meddled with relationships through love medicines, sterilization, and abortion; and they condoned divorce.

In effect, Handsome Lake and his followers sought to destroy the old kinship system by teaching people to value their spouse above everyone else. Just as the nuclear family was now to become the economic center of Indian life through its management of a family farm, it was also to become the moral and emotional center of both women's and men's lives. Male solidarity through warfare and the hunt was no longer possible. Therefore, the close ties of mothers and daughters also had to end.

By the end of the 18th century, acculturation seemed the only route to survival for the Iroquois and other eastern tribes. By abandoning many ancient patterns of behavior, Indians such as the Seneca were able to persevere into the 19th century. What Indian women thought of their new lives is unknown. Illiterate and struggling on a day-to-day basis to provide for their families, they did not keep a record of their feelings. Missionaries and federal agents, who were almost all men, wrote primarily about men's words and actions. Their papers reveal little about the trials of women as they faced a new world. Women's acceptance of the teachings of both the Quakers and Handsome Lake, however, did demonstrate their commitment to helping their people. In their desire to create a decent life for themselves and their children, they recognized the necessity for a new direction. Their recognition of this need signaled their strength, intelligence, and will to survive.

CHAPTER 6

PRAYER AND CHARITY: CREATING PUBLIC ROLES FOR MOTHERS

During the years of revolutionary turmoil, Americans paid less attention to the condition of their souls than to the state of their civil liberties. Clergymen worried about a "deadness" in the religious life of the nation and castigated their congregations for failing in their religious duties. By the 1790s many people felt a new urgency to turn their thoughts and energies back to the churches.

In this atmosphere the Second Great Awakening began, first in frontier areas long-starved for religious direction and then in the more densely settled regions of the East. (The first Great Awakening, a similar burst of religious fervor, had spread through the colonies over several decades beginning in the 1730s.) During the Second Great Awakening, religious revivals brought thousands of new converts into many different kinds of religious associations. Groups considered radical at the time, such as the Baptists and Shakers, grew dramatically in strength from the late 18th century to the mid-19th century, and established churches also expanded.

For women, the Second Great Awakening was a means of increasing their already significant religious influence. Women had long constituted the majority of worshipers in most churches. During the revivals, their numbers swelled to an even greater propor-

An engraving extolled the virtues of 18th-century womanhood. "A Virtuous Woman is a Crown to Her Husband," it said. By the late 18th century, American women were creating their own sphere of virtue.

The Shakers—known formally as the United Society of Believers in Christ's Second Appearing—were founded by Mother Ann Lee in 1774. The group took its name from the convulsive bodily movements that occurred during their worship. Women held leadership roles in the Society.

tion of the faithful. This growth ensured their dominance over the religious life of the nation.

Since the end of the 17th century, more women than men had sought solace in the churches for a variety of reasons. First, they had been socialized to sacrifice themselves for the good of others. Women therefore felt more comfortable with Christian teachings that promoted self-sacrifice. Second, because of the risks of childbearing, women faced death and permanent physical injury more often than men. Their frequent encounters with death led them to consider more seriously the state of their souls. (Not coincidentally, women often joined churches shortly after they married.) Perhaps equally important, women needed the comforts of religion to face the frequent deaths of their children and female friends. The infant mortality rate remained high throughout the 18th century, and every woman had friends or relatives who had died in childbirth or suffered injuries. These forces remained powerful incentives behind women's loyalty to their religious associations.

Female friendships and communal support of one another were a vital part of women's lives. In each town, and even in frontier areas whenever possible, women turned to each other for help in times of trouble. During childbirth and recovery, illness, and death, women needed the support of other women. Sometimes relatives helped, but often women needed to depend on their neighbors. As a

A Connecticut teenager, Prudence Punderson, depicted in this piece of needlework the journey from cradle to grave. Even young people were acutely conscious of the fragility of life; indeed, the artist died at 26.

result, female aloofness was rare in the 18th century. Women sought out the companionship of other women whenever possible, and the church was an important place to make connections. Membership in the same church gave women a claim to assistance they might not otherwise be able to make. Women's bonding, then, extended into and out of the churches. There, women could be confident of finding female friendship and respect as well as the fellowship of the faithful generally. The spiritual guidance of ministers was important, but so was membership in a female world of religious belief.

Ministers probably also won the support of female parishioners by teaching them that only through Christian principles had women been elevated to something resembling an equal standing with men. A theme that ran through many of the sermons delivered during the Second Great Awakening was the role of the churches in improving the social position of women. Only as a result of Christian instruction, the ministers argued, had men become willing to treat women with the respect they deserved. Other cultures and religions had not succeeded in raising the status of women, but Christianity, as one minister put it, had "exalt[ed] woman to an equal rank with man in all the felicities of the soul, in all the advantages of religious attainment, in all the prospects and hopes of immortality." It was therefore in the best interests of women to support the churches and the male ministers who led them.

George Whitefield preaches while holding a bag of cash in this 1760 satirical cartoon. As depicted here, women dominated most congregations, and ministers were dependent on them for support.

Although women were excluded from positions of leadership in most churches, ministers felt obliged to consider their needs and opinions when composing sermons, developing church policies, or administering church funds. Because women dominated the churches and made most of the donations to their collection plates, ministers increasingly were obliged to them for their own positions, status, and even salaries. Perhaps as a result, ministers' depictions of women softened in the 18th century. Gone was the old, Puritan emphasis on the decadent role of Eve in tempting Adam to sin. In its place appeared a gentler view of women as prudent, generous, and uniquely suited to religious duties. Good women, many ministers believed, were the main supporters of religion in their families and communities. Without them, Christians were in danger, as one minister explained in eulogizing his own mother: "At the Gap, which the Death of a wise and good Mother makes, does many times enter a Torrent of Impieties and Vices." Ministers often turned to Proverbs 31 for inspiration in teaching women about their domestic and social obligations:

> A good wife who can find? She is far more precious than jewels... She puts her hand to the distaff, and her hands hold the spindle. She opens her hand to the poor, and reaches out her hands to the needy.... She opens her mouth with wisdom and the teaching of kindness is on her tongue. She looks well to the ways of her household, and does not eat of the bread of idleness. Her children rise up and call her blessed; her husband also, and he praises her.

Sermons now portrayed the typical Protestant woman as a wise, hardworking matron with a keen desire to bring her children to Christ and perform charitable deeds.

The ministers' emphasis on female virtue complemented the republican belief that mothers were in a uniquely important position to promote the welfare of the nation. Like the politicians who argued that a republic's citizens needed to be moral, ministers believed that Christianity required personal virtue. Mothers were in the best position to teach their children the right moral lessons because early influences were regarded as the most important. Women's control over the nursery and the education of their children gave them the unique opportunity to instill youth with both proper Christian and proper republican qualities before other, less uplifting forces could interfere. In her defense of higher education for girls, Abigail Adams

The career of poet Phillis Wheatley (1754?-84) illustrates the close connection between religious devotion and female accomplishment in the 18th century. As the first woman of letters to comment on public affairs, Wheatley was renowned in revolutionary-era Boston for her intelligence, gentle demeanor, and piety. Her strong Christian faith and the patronage of evangelical women were essential to Wheatley's success.

Brought to America from Africa when she was about seven or eight years old, Wheatley demonstrated her keen intelligence and religious inclinations immediately. Within a year and a half, according to her master John Wheatley, she "attained the English Language ... to such a Degree as to read any, the most difficult Parts, of the Sacred Writings." Her temperament and accomplishments led her to be treated as a valued member of the wealthy and pious Wheatley family of Boston, even though she had been purchased by them as a slave. She became one of the best-educated women in late colonial Boston, even pursuing the study of Latin for a period of time.

Under the sponsorship of her mistress, Susanna Wheatley, Phillis Wheatley joined the Old South Meeting House and entered into a life of deep religious introspection, often expressed through her poetry. She published her first poem when she was 13, and at 16 was acclaimed for an elegy written upon the death of evangelical preacher George Whitefield. In 1773, at the age of 19, Wheatley published a book of verse, *Poems on*

Phillis Wheatley

Various Subjects, Religious and Moral.

Wheatley depended heavily on the patronage not only of Susanna Wheatley, but also of the Countess of Huntingdon, an Englishwoman active in evangelical and antislavery circles. The countess paid for the publication of the Whitefield elegy and of *Poems.* She also introduced Wheatley to various literary and government figures during a brief trip to England in 1773. Their mutual bonds were religious faith and the belief that evangelical Christianity held the potential to improve the human condition.

Between 1773 and 1778 Susanna Wheatley, her husband John, and daughter Mary died. Suddenly the young poet was left without the financial support to continue publishing her work. She married John Peters in 1778, but he was a poor provider who tried several different professions, ranging from shopkeeping to medicine without success. Eventually, Wheatley was forced to support herself by working in a boardinghouse. Although she continued to write whenever she found the time, she had, for unknown reasons, lost the patronage of Boston society. Perhaps her marriage was regarded as unsuitable. More likely, evangelical leaders of both sexes probably believed that as a married woman, she should spend her time on domestic chores rather than poetry.

After Wheatley gave birth to three children in rapid succession, all of whom died in infancy, her health gave way. Seemingly forgotten by her early supporters, she died in poverty at only 30 years of age.

argued that intelligence in men could arise only from intelligence in women: "Much depends ... upon the early education of youth, and the first principles which are instilled take the deepest root." She concluded, "If we mean to have heroes, statesmen, and philosophers, we should have learned women."

The comments of minister William Lyman are further evidence of the faith Americans had come to place in maternal influence. In 1802 he wrote, "Mothers do, in a sense, hold the reigns of government and sway the ensigns of national prosperity and glory. Yea, they give direction to the moral sentiments of our rising hopes and contribute to form their moral state. To them therefore our eyes are turned." Just as politicians promoted the maternal role, ministers elevated mothers' lessons to a plane equal or even superior to their own. In mothers' hands rested not only the future of the nation, but that of the churches as well.

Women received high praise for their work as mothers, but unfortunately motherhood was virtually the only vehicle through which 18th-century women could earn social recognition. Other avenues of public service remained closed to them. They could not participate directly in the political life of the new United States, for they could neither vote nor hold public office. Their property rights were severely restricted by law, so they had difficulty participating in commerce. The occupations open to women were generally menial ones. The few that were respectable—healer, midwife, and teacher—were all extensions of a mother's role in caring for her family. Some women with intellectual gifts were beginning to exercise influence through their writings, but most could not hope to imitate their example. No college had opened its doors to women, and therefore only those whose fathers arranged for their private instruction could hope to rival educated men in intellectual pursuits. If they did receive the equivalent of a college-level education, they risked social ridicule; highly learned women in general earned reputations for eccentricity.

Faced with these daunting limitations on their lives, women made a social virtue out of necessity. Using their influence in the churches, they succeeded in creating a public role from their private work in the home. Beginning in the 1790s, churchwomen founded a variety of self-help and charitable societies that, over the years, exerted a wide social influence. Through maternal associations, charitable organizations, and reform societies, individual women came to wield significant power.

No such opportunities had existed for colonial women. Female associations did not exist before the Revolution. Women came together to pray, but their groups were informal and single-minded in purpose. Charitable work was conducted only by individuals, local ministers, and the all-male Overseers of the Poor. Generally, men told women what to do for the poor, or matrons decided privately to assist specific people. Group efforts would have been perceived as usurpations of men's authority. Women were not regarded as capable administrators. Ironically, public recognition of the importance of motherhood—that most private of domestic obligations—gave women their first opportunity to find fulfillment outside the home. As mothers, women were permitted to form associations to further their important work. Maternal societies (the first mothers' clubs) attracted many women. Initially intended to help women become better mothers, many eventually became charitable or reform societies as well.

Women also turned to churches to find new avenues for effecting social change. Under the sponsorship of ministers, churchwomen created some of the first significant public roles for their sex. Although female religious associations were largely a 19th-century phenomenon, their foundation was laid by religious women of the colonial period.

The work of Rebecca Gratz (1781–1869) is illustrative of the kind of influence women could exert through charitable and religious work. It also demonstrates that Jewish as well as Christian women promoted reform and worked to create good public institutions for the sick and the poor. Gratz lived in Philadelphia and commanded both personal wealth and family prestige. At 20 she was already committed to charity work and helped establish one of the city's first female relief societies, the Female Association for the Relief of Women and Children in Reduced Circumstances. She served as its first secretary. As a mature woman, Gratz, who never married, was instrumental in founding numerous other charities, including the Philadelphia Orphan Asylum, the Female Hebrew Benevolent Society, the Jewish Foster Home and Orphan Asylum, the Fuel Society, the Sewing Society, and the Hebrew Sunday School Society. This

Rebecca Gratz, a celebrated Philadelphia beauty, never married. She devoted her life to charitable work.

last was probably her most significant accomplishment. The first such organization of its kind in the nation, it served as a model for all subsequent Jewish Sunday schools. Her work earned her the praise, admiration, and gratitude of Philadelphians.

Gratz's life reveals the new roads to significant social activism that were becoming available to women at the beginning of the 19th century. Although few women could match Gratz's energy and influence, many imitated her spirit in their own benevolent activities. Significantly, women found their greatest strength in working together. Colonial women gave their 19th-century descendants a legacy of strong female friendships, a tradition that proved essential for women's new social roles.

In fact, the earliest formal women's associations probably grew out of informal religious meetings women sponsored in their homes. Women long had gathered together for prayer and religious discussions. Throughout the 18th century these meetings served as intellectual and social outlets as well as spiritual ones. At the turn of the century women began to convert their prayer meetings into more ambitious associations. The example of the Female Religious and Cent Society of Jericho Center in Vermont was probably typical. Initially, this group of women met to pray out of a desire to "do good" and express their collective support for religion. Soon they were raising money for the missionary movement, a popular cause in the early 19th century.

In order to conduct their business properly, the Vermont women decided in 1806 to write up articles to govern their society. They proclaimed that the members would meet every other week "for social prayer and praise and religious instruction and edification ... [and that] all persons attending the meeting shall conduct themselves with seriousness and solemnity dureing the Exercises nor shall an Illiberal remark be made respecting the performance of any of the members, neither shall they report abroad any of the transactions of the society to the prejudice of any of its members." They insisted that members adhere to a strict code of mutual support in their efforts to improve the religious life of the country. In a culture that still questioned every attempt by women to gain a public voice, a united front was necessary to gain acceptance. Female solidarity was essential if they were to expand their horizons beyond the fireside.

Women who joined together to promote religious and charitable causes sought primarily to improve the human condition, not their own status. That the two went hand in hand may have gone unnoticed at first. Their efforts seemed in concert with traditional belief in women's potential to do good and help others. Only later, when women already had carved out a major sphere of influence in charity work, did ministers and politicians begin to fear what they had helped to create. In idealizing motherhood, men had opened the way for the higher education of girls and the group activities of mature women. Both experiences provided women with the tools and the confidence they needed to seek control over their own lives. Within a few decades some American women were arguing that as moral beings, they had the right to a political voice. At that point there was no returning to their colonial forebears' standard of female conduct. Women activists had found a voice and the will to express it.

Many women applied their domestic skills and interests in working for orphanages and other charities to benefit needy women and children. Harriet Sewall painted this image of an orphanage.

CHRONOLOGY

1754–63	French and Indian War
1763	Pontiac's Rebellion
April 19, 1775	Battles of Lexington and Concord; American Revolution begins
July 4, 1776	Declaration of Independence signed
1776	New Jersey Constitution gives women the right to vote
1776–77	British army wages successful campaigns against American troops in New Jersey and New York
September 1777	Philadelphia, Pennsylvania, falls to the British
October 1777	British defeated at Saratoga, New York
1777–1804	Northern states abolish slavery
1779	British launch campaigns in the South
Summer 1780	Ladies Association raises funds for American army
October 19, 1781	British army surrenders at Yorktown, Virginia
1783	Treaty of Paris ends the American Revolution
1787	United States Constitution ratified; slave trade begins to expand; Philadelphia Young Ladies' Academy founded
1790	Iroquois's relocation to reservations completed; Second Great Awakening begins
1790s	First women's charitable and reform societies formed
1799	Seneca religious leader Handsome Lake begins preaching to the Iroquois
1807	New Jersey election law denies women the right to vote
1808	Slave trade ends in accordance with Article 1, Section 9, of the U.S. Constitution

FURTHER READING

A Note on Sources

In the interest of readability, the volumes in this series include no discussion of historiography and no footnotes. As works of synthesis and overview, however, they are greatly indebted to the research and writing of other historians. The principal works drawn on in this volume are among the books listed below.

General Women's History

Axtell, James. *The Indian Peoples of Eastern America: A Documentary History of the Sexes.* New York: Oxford University Press, 1981.

Buel, Joy Day, and Richard Buel, Jr. *The Way of Duty: A Woman and Her Family in Revolutionary America.* New York: W.W. Norton, 1984.

Clinton, Catherine. *The Plantation Mistress: Woman's World in the Old South.* New York: Pantheon, 1982.

Cott, Nancy F. *The Bonds of Womanhood: "Woman's Sphere" in New England, 1780–1835.* New Haven: Yale University Press, 1977.

De Pauw, Linda Grant, and Hunt, Conover. *Remember the Ladies: Women in America, 1750–1815.* New York: Viking Press in association with The Pilgrim Society, 1976.

Hoffman, Ronald, and Albert, Peter J., eds. *Women in the Age of the American Revolution.* Charlottesville: University Press of Virginia for the United States Capitol Historical Society, 1989.

James, Janet Wilson. *Changing Ideas about Women in the United States, 1776–1825.* New York: Garland, 1981.

Jensen, Joan M. *Loosening the Bonds: Mid-Atlantic Farm Women, 1750–1850.* New Haven: Yale University Press, 1986.

Kerber, Linda K. *Women of the Republic: Intellect and Ideology in Revolutionary America.* Chapel Hill: University of North Carolina Press, 1980.

Kerber, Linda K., and Jane Sherron De Hart, eds. *Women's America: Refocusing the Past,* 3rd ed. New York: Oxford University Press, 1991. Part I: "Traditional America, 1600–1820."

Klinghoffer, Judith Apter, and Elkis, Lois. "'The Petticoat Elector': Women's Suffrage in New Jersey, 1776–1807." *Journal of the Early Republic* 12 (Summer 1992): 159–193.

Norton, Mary Beth. *Liberty's Daughters: The Revolutionary Experience of American Women, 1750–1800.* Boston: Little, Brown, 1980.

Norton, Mary Beth, and Carol Ruth Berkin, eds. *Women of America: A History.* Boston: Houghton Mifflin, 1979. Part II: "Colonial America to 1800."

Salmon, Marylynn. *Women and the Law of Property in Early America.* Chapel Hill: University of North Carolina Press, 1986.

Scholten, Catherine M. *Childbearing in American Society: 1650–1850.* New York: New York University Press, 1985.

Spruill, Julia Cherry. *Women's Life and Work in the Southern Colonies.* 1938. Reprint. New York: W.W. Norton, 1972.

Swan, Susan Burrows. *Plain and Fancy: American Women and Their Needlework, 1750–1850.* New York: Holt, Rinehart and Winston, 1977.

Ulrich, Laurel Thatcher. *A Midwife's Tale: The Life of Martha Ballard, Based on Her Diary, 1785–1812.* New York: Knopf, 1990.

The Revolutionary Era

Bailyn, Bernard. *Ideological Origins of the American Revolution.* Cambridge: Harvard University Press, 1967.

Countryman, Edward. *The American Revolution.* New York: Hill and Wang, 1985.

Gross, Robert A. *The Minutemen and Their World.* New York: Hill and Wang, 1976.

Isaac, Rhys. *The Transformation of Virginia, 1740–1790.* Chapel Hill: University of North Carolina Press, 1982.

Morgan, Edmund S. *The Birth of the Republic, 1763–1789.* Rev. ed. Chicago: University of Chicago Press, 1977.

Nash, Gary B. *The Urban Crucible: Social Change, Political Consciousness, and the Origins of the American Revolution.* Cambridge: Harvard University Press, 1979.

Royster, Charles. *A Revolutionary People at War: The Continental Army and American Character, 1775–1783.* Chapel Hill: University of North Carolina Press, 1979.

Wood, Gordon S. *The Creation of the American Republic, 1776–1787.* New York: W.W. Norton, 1969.

Cultural and Social History

Ahlstrom, Sydney. *A Religious History of the American People.* Garden City, N.Y.: Image Books, 1975.

Berlin, Ira, and Hoffman, Ronald, eds. *Slavery and Freedom in the Age of the American Revolution.* Charlottesville: University Press of Virginia for the United States Capitol Historical Society, 1983.

Cremin, Lawrence A. *American Education: The Colonial Experience, 1607–1783.* New York: Harper & Row, 1970.

———. *American Education: The National Experience, 1783–1876.* New York: Harper & Row, 1980.

Gilmore, William J. *Reading Becomes a Necessity of Life: Material and Cultural Life in Rural New England, 1780–1835.* Knoxville: University of Tennessee Press, 1989.

Graymont, Barbara. *The Iroquois in the American Revolution.* Syracuse, N.Y.: Syracuse University Press, 1972.

Gutman, Herbert G. *The Black Family in Slavery and Freedom, 1750–1925.* New York: Pantheon, 1976.

Innes, Stephen, ed. *Work and Labor in Early America.* Chapel Hill: University of North Carolina Press, 1988.

Jennings, Francis. *Empire of Fortune: Crowns, Colonies and Tribes in the Seven Years War in America.* New York: W.W. Norton, 1988.

Jordan, Winthrop D. *White Over Black: American Attitudes Toward the Negro, 1550–1812.* Chapel Hill: University of North Carolina Press, 1968.

Kulikoff, Allan. *Tobacco and Slaves: The Development of Southern Cultures in the Chesapeake, 1680–1800.* Chapel Hill: University of North Carolina Press, 1986.

Lockridge, Kenneth A. *Literacy in Colonial New England: An Enquiry into the Social Context of Literacy in the Early Modern West.* New York: W.W. Norton, 1974.

Mullin, Gerald W. *Flight and Rebellion: Slave Resistance in Eighteenth-Century Virginia.* New York: Oxford University Press, 1972.

Nash, Gary B. *Forging Freedom: The Formation of Philadelphia's Black Community, 1720–1840.* Cambridge: Harvard University Press, 1988.

Pierson, William. *Black Yankees: The Development of an Afro-American Subculture in Eighteenth-Century New England.* Amherst: University of Massachusetts Press, 1988.

Silverman, Kenneth. *A Cultural History of the American Revolution.* New York: Thomas Y. Crowell, 1976.

Smith, Daniel Blake. *Inside the Great House: Planter Family Life in Eighteenth-Century Chesapeake Society.* Ithaca, N.Y.: Cornell University Press, 1980.

Sobel, Mechal. *The World They Made Together: Black and White Values in Eighteenth-Century Virginia.* Princeton: Princeton University Press, 1987.

Wallace, Anthony F.C. *The Death and Rebirth of the Seneca.* New York: Vintage, 1972.

Zilversmit, Arthur. *The First Emancipation: The Abolition of Slavery in the North.* Chicago: University of Chicago Press, 1967.

Primary Sources Cited in the Text

Condict, Jemima. *Jemima Condict, Her Book: Being a Transcript of an Essex County Maid During the Revolutionary War.* Newark, N.J.: Carteret Book Club, 1930.

Earle, Alice Morse, ed. *Diary of Anna Green Winslow: A Boston School Girl of 1771.* Boston: Houghton Mifflin, 1894.

A Girl's Life Eighty Years Ago: Selections from the Letters of Eliza Southgate Bowne. With an Introduction by Clarence Cook. New York: Scribners, 1887.

Greene, Jack P., ed. *The Diary of Landon Carter of Sabine Hall, 1752–1778.* 2 vols. Charlottesville: University Press of Virginia, 1965.

Jackson, John W., ed. *Margaret Morris: Her Journal with Biographical Sketch and Notes.* Philadelphia: George S. MacManus, 1949.

Karlson, Carol F., and Laurie Crumpacker, eds. *The Journal of Esther Edwards Burr, 1754–1757.* New Haven: Yale University Press, 1984.

Parkman, Ebenezer. Diary. Parkman Family Papers. American Antiquarian Society, Worcester, Mass.

Tayler, Mary Hunt. *The Maternal Physician: A Treatise on the Nurture and Management of Infants.* New York: Isaac Riley, 1811.

Wallett, Francis G., ed. *The Diary of Ebenezer Parkman, 1703-1782. First Part: Three Volumes in One, 1719-1755. With a Foreword by Clifford K. Shipton.* Worcester, Mass.: American Antiquarian Society, 1974.

INDEX

Acknowledgments

Some historians' work was particularly important in shaping the material presented in this book. We know a great deal about the Iroquois, for example, because Anthony F. C. Wallace studied them so carefully. His book, *The Death and Rebirth of the Seneca,* provided most of the information on the Seneca included in Chapters 1 and 5. Information on enslaved women's work patterns comes from the research of Lois Green Carr and Lorena S. Walsh in "Economic Diversification and Labor Organization in the Chesapeake, 1650–1820." Mary Beth Norton discovered many of the primary sources employed in writing Chapter 3. Her book, *Liberty's Daughters,* contains the story of the Ladies Association as well as other important information on women's responses to the Revolution. In *Women of the Republic,* Linda K. Kerber first analyzed the role of republican motherhood in shaping life in the early United States. Her work was important in writing Chapter 4. The material on women's suffrage in New Jersey comes from the article by Judith Apter Klinghoffer and Lois Elkis, "The Petticoat Elector." Thanks to the research of David Grimstead, we better understand the life and work of Phillis Wheatley. His article "Anglo-American Racism and Phillis Wheatley's 'Sable Veil,' 'Length'ned Chain,' and 'Knitted Heart'" provided many of the ideas on Wheatley presented in Chapter 5. Other information on the lives of northern African Americans appears in Gary B. Nash, *Forging Freedom.* Nancy F. Cott first analyzed the activities of postrevolutionary women in charitable and religious societies. Her book *The Bonds of Womanhood* provided many of the ideas discussed in Chapter 6.

I dedicate this book to my husband, Joseph O'Rourke, for his intellectual and emotional support and in appreciation for the many hours of child care he gave during the production of the manuscript.

Picture Credits

Marylynn Salmon is the author of *Women and the Law of Property in Early America* and co-author of *Inheritance in America: From Colonial Times to the Present,* as well as numerous scholarly articles on early American women's history. Dr. Salmon is a research associate in the history department at Smith College.

Nancy F. Cott is Stanley Woodward Professor of history and American studies at Yale University. She is the author of *The Bonds of Womanhood: "Woman's Sphere" in New England 1780–1835, The Grounding of Modern Feminism,* and *A Woman Making History: Mary Ritter Beard Through Her Letters;* editor of *Root of Bitterness: Documents of the Social History of American Women;* and co-editor of *A Heritage of Her Own: Toward a New Social History of American Women.*